Lost on Skinwal'

LOS' ON SKINWALKER RANCH

THE TRUE STORY OF A PROPERTY GUARD AND HIS ENCOUNTER WITH THE PARANORMAL

ERICK T. RHETTS

Lost on Skinwalker Ranch

ALSO, BY ERICK T RHETTS:

THE MULEDEER CHRONICLES

SOPHIA

DARK TALES BEFORE SLUMBER

**SKINWALKER RANCH:
IN THE SHADOW OF THE RIDGE**

REVELATIONS: END

HUNGRY a random isolated event

THE SHADOW WALKERS

THE AIRFIELD

Lost on Skinwalker Ranch

Published by Prensa Tinta Azul

Copyright © 2014 by Erick T. Rhetts

All rights reserved under International and Pan American Copyright Conventions. Published by Tinta Azul Publishing. No part of this book may be reproduced or transmitted in any form whatsoever without prior written permission from the author.

Published in the United States of America

ISBN-13: 978-1502511331, ISBN-10: 1502511339

Cover by Erick T. Rhetts

Lost on Skinwalker Ranch

Chapters

1: The Interview

2: The Ranch

3: A Nocturnal Visit

4: Drums up on the Mesa

5: Outside My Window

6: Rare Currency

7: Someone's At the Door

8: Vanishing Coyotes

9: Awakened

10: Green and Purple In the Snow

11: These are not Coyotes

12: Half-Light

13: Little People

14: Found

15: The Medicine Man

Epilogue

Lost on Skinwalker Ranch

Prologue

I met Riley in Peru. Like Riley, I, too, am an ex-pat—at least for the time being. Technically, I have not renounced my United States citizenship, nor do I intend to. It's just that living in South America, at least in this part of it, is a totally different life style, and for a writer like myself, economically more feasible.

It was my vocation that brought Riley and I together professionally. Living in the same ex-pat community, we ran into each other on a routine basis, mostly around the plaza and curbside markets. However, it was at a local watering hole—a euphemism for bar or saloon—that we came to be friends in the social sense. We happen to share similar taste in libation.

One thing led to another, and once he found out that I did some writing, he, in a somewhat inebriated state, suggested he had a story that might make a good book. As most of what I do is writing for others—ghostwriting, coincidentally enough—given the topic, I, of course, was interested.

Prior to meeting Riley, I had never heard of Skinwalker Ranch, and although I have been involved in a number of fiction and fantasy projects, had no particular interest in the paranormal. That all changed after hearing what Riley had to say. Inebriated or not, I had no doubt he was telling me the truth—or at least what he believed to be the truth. That he retold it to me time and again during the writing process with variation not in the facts, but in accord with his emotions and feelings at the time, convinced me even more so. This was not a script he had memorized.

To best prepare myself, I got my hands on two books on the subject, one written quite recently and the other considered the first,

Lost on Skinwalker Ranch

and learned what I could of the background. From what I read, I provide the following overview:

Skinwalker Ranch is the name given to a piece of property in Utah. It was purchased from its principal owner by a man and wife who wished to raise cattle. Over the approximately two years that they lived there with their two children they experienced one strange and unexplainable event after the other, including UFO sightings, weird cryptids—animals for which nature has no answer, sentient orbs and other light anomalies, disappearing livestock and pets, disembodied voices and beings that seemed to materialize out of the air and vanish again in the same way.

Convinced that they and their children were in danger, the property was sold to a wealthy real estate and aerospace investor by the name of Bigelow with an intense interest in all things paranormal and extraterrestrial. In order to protect his interest and discourage thrill seekers and the curious from trespassing on his property, he hired a small security force to monitor its nearly 500 acres.

Riley was one of those security guards.

Like me, prior to his employment with Bigelow's industries, Riley had little to no knowledge of the ranch or its reputation. That was to change in short order.

This is his story.

Author's note

Riley, as was required of all security, signed a non-disclosure agreement as part of the conditions of his employment. For this reason, I have not used his real name or the actual names of any of the people he has included in his narrative. The details and facts have otherwise been unaltered.

Lost on Skinwalker Ranch

For my part, I acknowledged taking some liberty with and perhaps even embellishing some of the dialogue. After all, you can hardly expect Riley to have remembered every word of every conversation he had at that time.

For those readers who would like to get a more historical feel for the actual location, I recommend <u>Skinwalker Ranch, No Trespassing</u> (Skinner and Wallace, 2014). It is the more fact-based resource of those on the market and provides a broader history not only as to the ranch, but also the Native American influence and the applicable legends.

Lost on Skinwalker Ranch

1: The Interview

I have to admit that I'm no writer and that I received a little bit of help putting this story together. But that said, the story is all mine and every word of it is true. Whether you as the reader want to believe it, well, that's up to you. It doesn't change the fact that it happened and that it happened the way I tell it.

You might ask why I decided to tell it at all, and having decided to tell it, why now?

It's pretty simple, actually. I have read all the other books out there that talk about Skinwalker Ranch, including the one that just came out that allegedly has real people telling their stories, some of who say they were, at one time or another, employed at the ranch as security or lived there or somehow got on the property.

From what I have read in that book, I'm inclined to believe most of them. Either that, or they knew someone who really did, because the information they give is pretty much dead on. I know because I was one of them. Not one of the people who are in that book. No one came to me to ask me any questions, and although I had heard about the Wisconsin guy—we all did, I never met him and he never contacted me. I probably wouldn't have talked to him if he did. I consider myself a man of my word, and having signed the non-disclosure agreement, I would have had to honor it.

But that was five years ago, and since I'm no longer employed there, or with that organization, or the guy that heads it; and since it's pretty much a dead place, in terms of outside interest; and because, to tell you the truth, I'm hoping there's a few dollars in it, tight as things are these days, I thought I'd come forward (figuratively speaking) and tell what I went through. And from what I've read, it's a hell of a lot more of a story than the ones told by most everyone else.

But I'll let you decide that for yourself.

Lost on Skinwalker Ranch

I, too, was hired, back in 2009, as security for the company that owned the ranch. Actually, following my interview—which took place at the end of September, I thought I was only going to be assigned locally here in Nevada and welcomed it. Although I won't say from where exactly, I'm from just outside of Vegas and was living there when I got involved. I didn't tell anyone at the time, meaning the other guys working security and those that hired me, but I was living in a separate apartment in my parents' house. I kept it to myself that the wife had recently thrown me out. It's not a sad story.

I wish I could say that she caught me fooling around, or something like that. But the truth is we just weren't getting along too well. I guess you can say it was my fault; After 26 years, I was bored with the whole thing. She threatened to leave the kids with me—we have two of them—and go to her mother's at the other end of the state. I know this is going to sound horrible to some of you, but as I spent so much time away in the military: South America, Central America, the Middle East and parts of Europe, it wasn't like I was a big part of their lives, or they mine. The kids weren't little anymore and my wife had developed interests of her own. I told her she should stay in the house. It would just be easier that way, and so I left.

When the interview came about I was working part time in an electronics store, primarily selling cellphones and accessories. I had retired from military service—20 plus years—a little less than a year prior and had little ambition to do anything all that involved. A friend of mine gave me a call and told me about the position. At first, I wasn't all that interested. But after my wife and I split, I needed something to help me get my shit back together. Selling cellphones wasn't it. Plus, this friend of mine told me some things about Mr. Big and this place in Utah that sounded out there. I guess you can say my curiosity was piqued. I called the number he gave me and set up the appointment. They gave me an address to send the resume.

The interview was held in this building in an industrial park in Las Vegas, off of Tropicana. From the outside, it looked like it may have

Lost on Skinwalker Ranch

been a house at one time. They did some work to it, so now it's more like a professional building with offices and rooms like that. I met with some guy with an Irish accent. If you know the history of the ranch, you know who I'm talking about. If you don't, well then, it really doesn't matter. One guy with an Irish accent is as good as any other. He used the title of doctor instead of mister, but it wasn't a medical thing. He was educated. The other guy was a federal guy, used to be FBI or CIA, or some other collection of letters. Real serious guy, he was.

The interview started out pretty much like any other interview, with each side sort of feeling out the other. Most of the questions were mundane, where they ask about your experience and why you want the job, that kind of stuff. But then about half-way through, the doctor asks me what I think about UFOs. So I'm not really sure what he is asking.

"We have a need for people who are open-minded," he says.

Like I said, my friend had given me an idea as to what to expect, so I wasn't really surprised.

I look at his face and he's being serious and professional still. I look over at the other guy and he has the same look on his face. He's being serious, but not all hard and peering, nothing like that. "I can't say as I do or don't," I answer, and not flippant or sarcastic because I have the feeling these guys are being straight up. "I can't say that I've ever seen one."

The Irish guy then asks, "How about ghosts or spirits? What's your take on them?"

You have to understand at this time the only thing I knew about the Ranch was what my friend told me, so I knew it was supposed to be haunted, or something like that. But it wasn't like I went and looked up the place on the web. To tell you the truth, I didn't take it all that serious. But I'm playing it straight, as I can see this is really part of the interview. I was military police and I've been in some tough places and seen some strange shit, so I'm thinking they're

Lost on Skinwalker Ranch

testing me, my sanity or my ability to stay cool. My friend warned me it was different.

I took a chance. "I've had these dreams, if you want to call them that. They are like these repeating dreams. To me, they are ghosts or spirits. So, yeah, if that's what you mean. I believe there are entities that reveal themselves in different ways."

The federal guy says, "Go on."

Again, I look at their faces to see how serious they are and to see if I'm playing this right. My understanding is the job pays pretty well for security, and though my pension is okay—it pays the bills, if I'm going to be giving the soon to be ex-wife money and paying for my own place, I could use the boost in income. Plus, I needed something to do, something relevant.

"There's not all that much to it," I say, but since I'm telling the truth and I don't want them to think I'm making shit up, I explain it to them. "It's always the same, the dreams, the spirit, or ghost or whatever you want to call it, is always at the end of my bed. And it's as real looking as you can imagine, the room, everything. It's as if I am wide awake, as if I wake up and it's there, looming at the end of the bed. And I think that's what really messes me up. Because as far as I know, I am awake. That's what makes it so real. Anyway, I always strike out at it physically, and that's what really wakes me up. But it never makes a move toward me, just there looming. I perceive its presence as threatening; but like I said, it never does anything but stand there."

"What does it look like?" the Irish guy asks.

All I could do was shrug. "It's just a figure, but always male. Other than that, I can't give you any details. I'm sure it's clothed, things like that. But don't ask me to describe what it is wearing. I can't. And although at the time, I can see its face and features, not to the point of recall afterwards. All I can say is, it's life-like and as big as life. After I'm wakened by my own punching or kicking, it's gone and my heart is pumping. I have to lay back and tell myself to relax."

Lost on Skinwalker Ranch

"How often do you have these dreams?"

I have to admit his slight accent was a bit distracting and I was tempted to imitate him when I answered. "There's no routine to it," I tell him. "But often enough to make me think there's something to it. These incidents are different from regular dreams. There's no change to the scene and there's no storyline, as it were. It's just this thing, this figure—and always human—looming up at the end of the bed…and that's it."

The federal guy asked me what I thought it was. "You know, just humor me."

What else could I do but shrug? "I don't know. I think, if I had to give an answer, it's some sort of manifestation, some soul or spirit that has a connection to the property, something like that. Maybe something that has an attachment to me from a previous life."

The doctor's eyes widened at that one. "So you do believe, at least in some way, in the paranormal?"

Of course, I'm aware of the term and I think I know what he's asking, so I answered. "I'm not a religious guy, by any means, not the Heaven and Hell kind. But I do believe in a sort of collective conscious. I like to call it the antennae theory."

I could see that both were interested, but maybe I wasn't making it all that clear.

"People are like antennae. We're like televisions or radios that pick up this collective conscious like a signal. But as we all have slightly different programing, it comes across as different to us and so we project it differently." I didn't want to get too into it. I'm not sure they really wanted to hear it and I haven't really given it sufficient thought myself.

Anyway, I guess they had heard what they wanted to hear. The interview went on only a few more minutes after that and most of the rest was basic small talk. They said they had a couple more candidates to see that day and they would be in touch one way or the other.

Lost on Skinwalker Ranch

I received a call a few days later. It was early in the day, before noon. I had given them my cell number and the number to the land line in my apartment. But I made sure that if they were going to call, to call the cell. I didn't want to take the chance of them calling the house and someone other than me answering. No one wants to hire a guy whose life is showing some instability.

It wasn't the doctor or the federal guy that called, but some guy whose name I don't remember. He told me that if I was still interested, they'd like to offer me the position. Of course, I was, and so I went back to the Vegas office to do the paperwork and go over the details.

Once there, I was instructed to sign the non-disclosure agreement and provided some of the particulars. I was somewhat hesitant about the ranch part and so let on that I'd be okay with working locally, but I could also see that wasn't part of the plan. I was given a brief summary of Mr. Big, his business endeavors here in Vegas, his interest in the ranch in Utah and some of the stories related to it. However, I was also told that I would be assigned initially to Mr. Big's properties here in town, and that once I had completed the training, I would be spending two week stints at the ranch. They didn't say how long the job would last, and I didn't ask. I wasn't looking for a new career.

I'll skip the part about the local work. It was always at one of these two buildings owned by Mr. Big, and for the most part, it was boring stuff. Nothing exciting ever happened. It was more verifying who was coming in and out or checking people who entered the parking lots. To tell you the truth, I wasn't even sure what all the fuss was about. I knew the one place had these labs filled with all kinds of technology equipment and fancy computer rooms. They were doing some serious stuff with space stations; scientists and engineers were coming and going on a regular basis. But for me, the real story starts about three months later.

Lost on Skinwalker Ranch

2: The Ranch

I've already acknowledged that I knew nothing about the ranch when I went for the job. However, by the time I was given my first assignment there, I had gone through some specific training and had the chance to talk with some of the other guards. And that's the way the conversation always seemed—guarded, as if they thought they were being tested in some way. Besides that, however, each guy had a little something different to report. Most of it was about things they felt while on the property, like a sense of uneasiness or a vague sense of dread, or odd lights they'd seen; they called them orbs or auras. It depended on who was talking. They all said, though, that it was for the most part slow and boring, especially during the day, most of which, apparently, was spent napping. I was also told that it gets cold in the winter. All in all, it left me curious, but not apprehensive or scared, nothing like that.

The routine was, as I already said, a two week rotation. Two guys at a time would be assigned to the ranch, spend two weeks there on the property and then rotate out. By rotate out, I mean come back to Las Vegas and work the properties here, either at the headquarters or in the complex off Tropicana, west of the airport.

I was told that each rotation at the ranch could be with a different guy, but the word was it didn't always work out that way. There was no set pattern, not formally. More or less, it came down to who was available when. Most of the guys had families. Along the way, whether in Vegas or at the ranch, I worked with or at least met more than a dozen guys, and I'm sure I'm leaving out a couple: Bob, Tony, John, Mark, Nick, Chuck, Randy, Jason, Ryan, Carl, Greg, Kelly and Rocky. They all have last names, too; but I'm not going to give them. And the fact is, I've included my name also. Just to keep it all on the up and up.

Lost on Skinwalker Ranch

The company offered to provide me with a rental car to drive to the ranch, but I opted for the flight instead. We're talking more than 500 miles, closer to 550. They made arrangements for me to fly out of McCarran and into Vernal, Utah. That first time, I was picked up there by Mark and a woman. I had met Mark before while working in Las Vegas. We hadn't talked all that much, but we weren't new to each other. The woman appeared to be in her 60s. She was averaged sized with light brown hair and her bangs had these sort of blonde highlights, but nothing extreme. She wore glasses with large oval lenses and the more traditional rims. She introduced herself as Joan. She and her husband were the ranch caretakers.

It's around 20 miles from Vernal to the ranch. We made a couple of stops before we left the city to pick up some groceries. I was encouraged to select a few things for myself, all of which went on the company credit card. I included some adult beverage and met with no resistance.

This was not my first trip to Utah, but it was the first time that I had come this far north and east. For the most part, it is a godforsaken land. You can literally go miles along highway 40 without seeing a building or even a house worth mentioning, not one. It is nothing but scrub brush, rock, stones and dirt for as far as the eye can see, interrupted only by hills and ridges. I'm not saying the whole place is desolate or uninhabited, I'm saying it only seems that way…if it wasn't for the occasional car that goes by.

I saw my first cluster of houses as we were only a mile or so east of Fort Duchesne. And when I say cluster, I mean one here and one there. Nothing like a neighborhood. Even when we actually made the turn-off on 88 to head south and went past the actual city or town itself, there wasn't much in the way of anything. The whole population is like 700 people, and by the looks of it, you'd think they all live in the same house. That's obviously an exaggeration, but that's how few structures there are.

Lost on Skinwalker Ranch

To get to the actual ranch, we made a right onto 7500 E. It has a name, but isn't much of a road. It's more like a long driveway which runs east to west and practically up to the house. We passed the infamous East Gate along the way, but I didn't know it at the time. The paved part of the road ends just as you get on the ranch and becomes all dirt. There's a part that runs south and another that turns to the right. The south road leads to the south gate. The other way goes past some corrals and then continues west along the base of a ridge that runs along the north edge of the property. I think they call it Skinwalker Ridge. To the west end of the property, just before the dirt road ends, there are a couple of old, dilapidated buildings called the Old Homestead. It's the spookiest part of the ranch. There's another paved road beyond that, but it doesn't allow access to the property.

The only other property we passed on 7500 E worth mentioning belongs to this guy named Jon Garcia. His property borders the ranch to the east, although his house is all the way to the opposite end of the property and there's a pond between his place and the ranch. I would see him around now and then, mostly from a distance, and we never had the chance to talk.

The ranch house itself, where Joan and her husband live, sits within a grove of trees that sits less than a hundred feet inside and to the left of the main entrance. The driveway towards the house was also all dirt, worn by the continual passing of tires. It kicked up its fair share of dust as we drove over it and towards this trailer located to the right of the house and parallel to it. There was a walkway between the two houses and a narrow swath of lawn. The trailer was similar to the kind you see at construction sites, nearly as long as the house but not quite as wide. There was a second trailer, smaller and all white, off to the right and back among what looked to be a series of corrals.

Joan, who was driving, parked the SUV a short piece from the house and we grabbed up the packages, and me my duffel bag, and I followed Mark to the trailer. Joan made for the house. Once inside the trailer, Mark showed me to my room. I was glad I didn't have to

Lost on Skinwalker Ranch

share. That'd be awkward. The room had a bed and some sparse furnishings. There was a dresser, a work table and a night table with a lamp. I had no complaints. He showed me the kitchen and a bathroom with a shower. It was pretty much what you would expect from a trailer.

After I had unpacked and put my belongings in the dresser drawers, Mark took me for a walk around a bit of the property. I don't mind telling you it was cold, somewhere in the teens. I was dressed for the weather, but it didn't make all that much of a difference. Even with heavy duty gloves and doubled-up on the socks, my fingers and toes were feeling it.

We took a walk out to the East Gate. To get there we walked up passed those corrals and went back east, keeping to this path in the dirt that was to the north of 7500 E and ran along the base of a rise Mark referred to as the mesa. It took us a good 15-20 minutes to get there, probably a mile or so. It would have been easier to take the road, but Mark wanted me to get a feel for the place.

Gesturing towards the mesa, Mark said, "Some of this belongs to Mr. Big, but most of what's to the north belongs to the neighbor. But we have an arrangement that if there's someone up there, on ranch property or not, they are trespassing. Our job is to tell them to leave. If they won't, we have the right to detain them and we call the local police."

I couldn't imagine there'd be anyone who would want to be up there and said as much.

"There's some UFO types that try to get on the ranch," he told me, "but most of the time it's just local teens driving up to the gate. Usually, we shine a flashlight on them and they take off."

"What do they come here for?"

His tone was more annoyed than anything else. "Ghost stories. The locals think the place is haunted by spirits. Supposedly that's the reason Big bought the place, to get a firsthand look at whatever is out here. People say they see UFOs here all the time. The guy who sold it

Lost on Skinwalker Ranch

to him said he saw actual alien pilots and some sort of portal that opened up right before his eyes and out crawled these beings."

I tried to look like I was taking it all in stride, but I guess I wasn't all that convincing.

"You'll see. You'll be out with me here tonight with a camera taking pictures of the dark."

After that we turned around and went back past the trailer and corrals and up to the old homestead. It's an old house that was left to the elements and is definitely not inhabitable or something that can be renovated. Why no one has torn it down is beyond me. There's also a smaller structure that looks like it may have been a wood shed and another closer to the house that looks like storage of some sort. We peered into the main house. There were significant holes in the roof, parts of the white-washed walls had crumbled and the floor boards were almost completely rotted away.

As we walked back towards the road, Mark said, "Somewhere around here is where the guy and his wife saw that portal." He gestured vaguely out towards the fields.

As we got back out on the road, Mark pointed to a small shed-like structure that was among a cluster of trees to the right and on the other side from where the house was. He said he had seen some strange creature come slinking out of it one night which then ran off into the trees. There wasn't much left to it in the way of structure.

I am not ashamed to say, as he was telling me about it, I experienced a moment of closeness, as if my peripheral vision narrowed for just a second. It might not be the best way to describe it, but I don't know how else to explain it. Anyway, it passed real quickly, and as it was freezing, Mark suggested we go back.

That first night we did the patrol together, going out at about 10:00 pm. There is a pole with some lights there close to the house, but the rest of the place is dark and we had to rely on flashlights. We more or less took the same walk we had taken earlier, but this time we went up on the mesa. That was tough on the legs. I'm not in the same shape I

Lost on Skinwalker Ranch

used to be. Not only that, but the air was cold and with the deep breaths I was taking my lungs were burning.

Mark had brought a digital camera along and he had me stop here and there and he would take some photos. He'd then ask me if I was sensing anything or feeling anything.

When I asked him what it was I was supposed to be sensing, he said with a shrug, "Some guys say they feel a presence."

I didn't feel any presence. I felt cold.

He then gave me the camera and I took some shots of him. He told me not to do anything special, just make sure that he was in the middle of the shot and there was some room around him. So that's what I did.

We came down from the mesa, which was a pain in the ass in the dark. The footing can be tricky and at times loose pebbles and dirt give way and scare they shit out of you. I thought for sure I was going to go down more than once, but I managed to stay on my feet.

Once back on low ground, we walked along a narrow gulch which I imagined in the warmer weather was a shallow creek of some sort. Mark then found the path he was looking for and we went out to the East Gate. But it was quiet. There was nothing to see and no one around. After hanging around for a few minutes, Mark suggested we go check on the dogs which were inside the first dog run on the property. At that point, I didn't know what a dog run was, other than what it sounded like.

I was, of course, quick to learn that there were actually three dog runs in all. The first one was in the big open field to the west of the house, the second was beyond a thin grove of trees that separated the big field from the middle one. Then there was a third run in the field to the west. Each of the runs was more or less in the middle of the pasture and consisted of an area about seventy feet long and fifteen foot wide, surrounded by a six foot high chain link fence with a wood observation tower at one end. These were actually the infamous bait pens in which, supposedly, calves were tied to stakes in the ground

Lost on Skinwalker Ranch

and left as live bait to attract whatever was stalking the property and slaughtering the cattle.

That was something that must have taken place before I arrived. I didn't see any cattle on the property. The corrals were empty.

There in the first dog run, or bait pen, whichever you prefer, was a black lab named Rucca. She seemed happy to see us. Mark hooked her up to a leash that he had brought along and together the three of us walked back towards the trailer. The dog was friendly and came over to me repeatedly as we walked, mostly sniffing at my hand and allowing me to pet her. She came across as calm and well-trained.

There were two other dogs on the property. One was another lab and the other was a collie that belonged to Joan and her husband. Max, the other lab, was on a chain back by the trailer. Bella, the collie, I assume was at the house.

Back at the trailer, Mark told me to go on in and he took care of Rucca, chaining her up alongside Max. When he came in, I was already at the kitchen table and had put out two glasses and gone for the bottle of Jack Daniels. I wasn't in any way a big drinker, but I liked to have a couple of fingers at the end of the day, if you know what I mean. It wasn't a nightly thing, but probably more nights than not. Rarely did I ever go back for seconds, maybe only on weekends when I didn't have anything else to do.

I guess Mark didn't intend on joining me by the way he first looked at the two glasses on the table. He said afterwards he wasn't much of hard liquor guy, preferring the occasional beer. But at it was a cold night and he felt a bit of chill in his bones, why not? So I poured him a couple of fingers also. Both of us went neat—no ice.

While we were nursing the Jack, he brought out the camera and we took a look at the few dozen photos we had taken. Most of them were of no real interest, but there were a few with these spots of bluish light in them. Mark called them orbs and said it was just one of the things we were looking for and that we would have to include them in our daily reports.

Lost on Skinwalker Ranch

I'll describe what I saw, but it's nothing all that thrilling. Here and there in 8 or 9 of the photos were multiple spherical-like orbs, more like spots of light. They definitely seemed to have some dimension to them, though, meaning more like balls than simply flat circles. But I couldn't tell if the light they were giving off was a reflection or if it was something inside of them. Either way, you could barely make them out, almost as if they were mostly transparent. What I'm saying, is they weren't really bright in color or so clearly dimensional that you could say without doubt that they were actually there. To me, if there was a gun to my head, I'd say they were dust particles or some kind of particle that the camera was picking up. I know that when we were taking the pictures, I didn't notice any of these spots floating around at the time.

Mark counted the number of photos that had these spots, these orbs, and how many were in each and jotted the information down in a pad that he had. "All you have to do," he said, "when you make your report is put down the same information. It's what they expect."

Lost on Skinwalker Ranch

3: A Nocturnal Visit

That first week on the ranch was nothing special, the first few days, anyway. As far as anything strange, I didn't see anything or hear anything that I would say was paranormal or supernatural or that had anything to do with UFOs. We continued to take photos with the digital camera, and I continued to pretend to get excited whenever we caught orbs. By that third night, I had learned that any color other than blue was a cause for celebration and I made sure to make note of these events in my daily reports. Orange and red were the big time colors. The people back in Vegas thought these were more significant than the blue ones. I figured out on my own that red and orange were thought to be stronger, have more of an influence on people. I didn't feel anything special either way. I was pretty much convinced that the difference in the color had to do with the difference in whatever the ambient light was that particular night and how it was picked up by the camera lens.

As for regular earthly occurrences, I had my first encounter with uninvited guests that first Friday night. I had been up on the mesa, probably only my second time—Mark preferred to go up there, when I noticed what looked to be a splash of light down below and in the direction of the East Gate. I stayed up on the mesa and made my way in that direction. I wasn't all that far away. The light stayed steady so I was sure it was a couple of flashlights and not enough of a beam to be headlights.

As you get to the eastern part of the mesa, there's a way down that's fairly easy to navigate. So I went down and made my way over to this short foot bridge, I guess you'd call it—it's little more than plywood, and came to a stop on the other side of the culvert. But from where I was standing I had lost the light; either that or whoever was looking around heard me coming down the mesa and turned

Lost on Skinwalker Ranch

them off. I stood and listened to hear if there was anything stirring about, but there was a bit of a breeze and all I could hear was wind tapping through the branches and passing overhead.

With nothing else to do, I walked all the way over to the East Gate staying to the path. If there was anyone nosing around, I wanted them to see me. Mark, on the other hand, says he likes to stay to the trees and try to sneak up on whosoever there. My understanding is, more often than not, it's just local kids or curiosity seekers hoping to get a look of something spooky or have bragging rights to say they actually stepped on the property.

When I got up to the gate I heard the unmistakable sound of footsteps on the hard ground. I'd say there were two, maybe three people. But they were up the road and all I heard after that was car doors closing and the tires catching traction on the dirt as they took off. They must have kept the car lights off because I didn't see anything. I made note of the time on my watch so I could enter the encounter in my log. It was 23:47. That's thirteen minutes to midnight for regular people. We were supposed to let the local police know so they could keep a record. I let Mark worry about that; I was the new guy.

Following that little adventure, I started towards the west end of the property. I used my walkie-talkie to make contact with Mark to see if he had headed out that way or had gone down toward the South Gate. He told me he was out by the first dog run with Max. I was supposed to have Rucca with me, but the stupid dog went after a porcupine the night before and got stuck pretty good in the paw with a half dozen needles. Joan pulled them out—it was something she was used to—but Rucca was going to be out of commission a day or two until the swelling went down.

Along the dirt road in the direction of the old homestead there's a heavy duty tractor, the color faded from weathering. It just sits there. At least, I never saw anyone use it. For me it's a landmark. I know that once I get there, about a hundred feet or so and I'll be across

Lost on Skinwalker Ranch

from the first dog run and then another hundred feet or so and the road turns south to go west.

That night as I came up to the tractor there was this humming sound that caught my attention. It sounded like it was coming from up over the ridge to the north, but sometimes it's hard out there to tell where sounds originate from. I think it has to do with the bedrock, the ridge, the different heights all around, the nooks and crevices and the open land between. It's like one big resonance chamber. The sounds get knocked and bounced around and I swear you can even feel it vibrating beneath your feet.

Well, that humming just started to get louder and louder to the point where I was looking to take cover somewhere. I thought for sure something was coming down on my head. I would almost describe it as similar to an approaching train, the intensity I mean, not the actual sound. After a short while, the sound piqued and stayed steady for a minute or two, and then as if going wherever it was going, it started to lose that intensity, fell back to a hum and faded to where I was straining to hear it before I realized it had stopped.

I pushed the talk button on my walkie-talkie and cued up Mark. "Did you hear that?"

He called it a sizzle.

"Yeah, if that's what you want to call it."

I could hear him laugh. "Pretty loud isn't it? It's the power lines. That's the first time you've heard that out here?"

It was. "I'm sure if I had heard that before I would have said something."

"You'll get used to it. Something to do with the insulation of the wires. At least that's what I've been told. It's old and worn. The power current vibrates through the towers and right through the ground."

"As long as it's just the sound," I said to him, "and not the juice."

His walkie-talkie crackled and I missed what he said. I asked him to go again. "I said I'm going to leash up Max and I'll meet you over by the homestead. Give me about fifteen minutes or so."

Lost on Skinwalker Ranch

That was okay by me. That place is creepy at night, especially since he told me about that thing he saw coming out of the second house. I gave him the ten-four and set back out on the path.

One of the reasons for doing the patrol with the dogs is that they sense things before we do, especially the presence of coyotes and deer. I'm not too worried about the deer. They usually know we're there before we know about them and go leaping off. We rarely ever see them up close and only hear their steps or the sound they make as they pass through the brush.

It's the coyotes I am not too psyched about. One or two of them is not a big deal. But get three or four of them together and they could be an issue. I had yet to get close to any of them, but you can hear them in the dark, yipping or yelping back and forth to each other. Like I said, sounds out here are sometimes difficult to distinguish when it comes to distance, but you can still tell when the coyotes are far off and when their curiosity is getting the better of them. I felt safe on the path. There's not much cover there. But once you get out into the pastures, into the fields, it's not the same feeling. That's why Mark was coming across with Max.

I kept to a leisurely stride. It's not like there's anything else to do. We'd finish up the patrol and then go back to the trailer, maybe watch a movie or catch up on the news. We had cable. And I know I was going to warm up my insides with a couple of fingers of Jack, one for each hand. Not that I need it, but it's a good way to nod off once I'm ready to call it a night.

All I had for light was my flashlight. I kept the beam out in front of me so that I could see where I was walking. It is quite a distance from the tractor to the old homestead, more than half a mile given the way the road bends and curves. There was always the chance I would meet up with Mark along the way. He would head west across the pasture and pick up the road a few hundred yards out from the homestead. I kept my ears open for the sound of Max.

Lost on Skinwalker Ranch

I'd say I was about half way to where I was headed when I heard pebbles and dirt cascading down the ridge to my right. The sound was continuous, so I immediately thought there was something there. If a single rock had succumbed to gravity, it would have tumbled and brought some loose dirt with it, but the noise would have been short-lived. But this sound kept at it for longer than that. I stopped and shone the light in the direction it was coming from and just then the noise stopped. I painted the slope of the ridge with the beam, but I didn't see anything. I thought maybe it was something small, some animal, and that the light caused it to go still and hunker down in some crevice or behind some rock. Most of the time, you don't even see these critters in the broad day light until you come up on them and then they scatter. So not seeing it at night was no surprise.

I spent another few seconds looking and then started walking again. I don't think I made it more than 30 feet and whatever it was, it was back moving and heading down the ridge. I gave a quick turn and while walking backwards let the light bounce from one place to the next. I didn't see anything, but whatever it was, I heard it making noise as it came in my direction. And then it stopped. I stood still trying to look among the shadows there along the base of the ridge and among the brush and rocks. I decided if it was that small that I couldn't see any sign of it, it was nothing to worry about. "You're out in the middle of the desert, you idiot," I reminded myself and turned around again in the direction I was walking.

Mark and Max got to the homestead before I did. He must have made tracks across the pasture because he had just as far to go as I did, more or less.

"What took you so long?" he asked as Max came up and nuzzled up against my knees.

I told him about the noise. He said it was probably a rabbit. "They burrow up in the rocks and come down at night. I've seen them quite a few times before."

Lost on Skinwalker Ranch

We left the homestead, not that we went inside it or even over to it. Mark had been waiting for me over by the grove that was on the south side of the road. We walked west along the path and as far as the third dog run. We didn't usually go any further than that, not without the SUV. According to Mark there wasn't much activity on that end of the property. "Too far from the vantage points," he had said. Whatever that meant.

By the time we made it back to the trailer it was a little after two in the morning. And although it was cold outside, all of that walking works up a sweat beneath the layers of clothing so that the only part of you that feels any of the cold is the tip of your nose and the ears— if you don't have them covered. I was wearing a wool hat, so I didn't have that problem. But the tips of my fingers were a bit numb, even with the gloves on.

Mark passed on the Jack—go figure, so I decided on just the one glass. We watched some of the news and talked some football. Mark was a big fan. I could take it or leave it, but I guess I am a bit of a Seattle fan, and maybe Denver. I went in to crash right around 3:00.

The Jack gave me a warm buzz and all that walking in the cold air must have sapped me a bit, because no sooner had I pulled the blanket under my chin, I was out like a light.

With my eyes closed against the darkness of the room, I had that intense feeling that I was not alone and that someone was looking at me. I let my eyes open, fully expecting there'd be nothing there. The way I say it, though, doesn't do it justice. It makes it seem like there was this noticeable time expanse between the realization and opening my eyes. But there wasn't. Everything happened in an adrenalin-filled second or two.

The truth is when I first looked, my eyes were still closed because I was still sleeping. It was in a dream that I saw the figure standing at the end of my bed, tall and thin and grinning in a way that lacked any hint of humor.

Lost on Skinwalker Ranch

What woke me was the violent kicking of my right foot aimed in my sleep out toward the figure. But as I was under the covers, I wasn't able to kick out all that far. At the same time, I yelled out, "What are you doing here?" —or something like that.

Of course, when I did all that, I actually woke up and there was nothing there. The room was essentially dark with just the slightest bit of pale light visible at the bottom of the door. There must have been a light on out towards the kitchen. My heart was pumping like a drum and I had that shaky intensity you feel in your whole body when that much adrenalin is squirted through your veins all at once. I told myself it was just a dream—the kind I've had before—and laid my head back on the pillow.

4: Drums up on the Mesa

I went out to the kitchen for coffee that morning—my routine before taking a shower—and Mark, looking up from his own cup, said, "Late night visitor?"

It wasn't that I had completely forgotten about my episode, but I had no reason to believe he would know anything about it. "Come again."

"You yelled out something last night. More this morning, actually—it wasn't quite 4:00. Sounded like you were chasing someone away."

No reason denying it. "Oh, you heard that? A dream of sorts; I have them every now and then; this same one, I mean."

He looked as if he was expecting me to say more.

So I gave him a glimpse of it. "I'm dreaming that someone is in the room. And I swear, I see them as clear as day. It is always so unbelievably real. It's fucked up. I think I'm actually awake, but I'm awake in my sleep. This thing standing there startles the shit out me. In my dream, I physically strike out it, kicking and punching. Which I'm actually doing and which then wakes me for real. Of course, I'm all alone. There's no one there. I guess I yelled out before I woke up. Sorry if I woke you up."

He shook his head. "You didn't. I was just going in to bed myself. The funny thing is, when I passed your room, and I know you're going to think I'm pulling your leg, I had this feeling there was something or someone in there with you." He held his hands up in front of him as if he was showing me he was for real.

It made me laugh, in a good way. "Next time, don't be shy. Come in and take a look. Maybe you'll chase it away before I give myself the heart attack."

Lost on Skinwalker Ranch

After I came out of the shower, I had some oatmeal with Aunt Jemima make-believe maple syrup for breakfast and a second cup of coffee. I thought I could use the steam in my blood. It had snowed earlier that morning, and in fact, it was still coming down in a lazy flurry. It was the first snow they had out there since just before Christmas, according to Mark. It must have been falling at a pretty steady clip before we got up because there was already three or four inches on the ground. I opened the door of the trailer to have a look around and was surprised at the temperature. It was cold, but not as cold as the night before. Still two-pairs of socks weather, I decided. Although most of the bullshit took place at night, meaning teenagers and vehicles at the gates, we still had our rounds to do during the day.

It was after 10:00 when we went out together. We decided to take a walk down to the South Gate first, then come back a bit and cut across the pastures and go out to where the far dog run was. I called it field three. The plan after that was to walk the road below the ridge back to the trailer. Depending on how things looked, we would decide then whether to go out towards the East Gate. But like I said, no one unexpected comes down the road in day light. It's not spooky enough.

To the southern extreme of the property there is this gulch that winds out of the west and just keeps going all the way east and south. It's fairly wide at some points, but never gets all that deep from what I saw. Although frozen with the cold, I have been told that when the water is flowing, there are those that will get around the no trespassing signs by standing in the middle of the creek. It lets them get an unobstructed view of the property. Personally, I don't see the attraction. There's a bit of rise this side of the gulch, so there's no great sight line. And if they come out of the creek and climb up the ridge, well, then they are trespassing.

Anyway, when we got down there, Mark spotted these pretty weird footprints in the snow. They led down the rise and towards the creek. He stood alongside of the nearest one and bent down towards it to get a closer look. "Ever seen anything quite like this?" he asked.

Lost on Skinwalker Ranch

I had to admit, no.

They weren't all that distinct, having surrendered some of their depth and shape to the snow that was still falling. But there was enough of them still there that they could not have been left all that long ago. Mark called them hour-glass shaped. But that's not how I saw them. To me they looked more like someone had pressed bowling pins into the snow. Not the real kind. They'd be too big. More like those plastic ones that kids set up on the basement floor or out on the patio. The neck part, assuming the tracks led to the creek and not away from it, which was definitely the case, was to the back of the print and the fat part to the front. It was wider and more rounded to the middle and tapered where the toes would be. But there was no toe shape or anything like claws or nails. It was pretty much rounded.

I wear 9.5 shoes. My boots—made by Michelin—leave a bigger print than, say, if I was wearing sneakers. Their tread is heavier and they have steel toes. These prints were almost as long and not quite as wide. The really strange thing, though, is that they were about four feet apart, and whatever was making them was walking upright. There were only two sets of tracks.

It was also kind of funny that we didn't notice them earlier as we were making our way down here. These seemed to just pop up suddenly. Mark said it was the way the snow blows up depending on the direction of the wind, how fast the snow is falling and where the rock and trees are. It made sense to me.

"So what makes them?" I asked, truly curious. Because if it was an animal, it was no animal I had ever seen, not walking upright with bowling pin-shaped feet and a stride four feet long.

He straightened up from over the print we were looking at and grinned. "They don't call this place Skinwalker Ranch for nothing."

Keep in mind this was before I know what I know now.

By then I was aware that a couple of books had been written about the place. One was by the Irish guy that hired me; he and some other guy I hadn't met. And there was another one by some local guy who,

Lost on Skinwalker Ranch

from what I was told, saw some religious significance in the place. I hadn't read either one of them. Mark told me that there was some sort of Native American legend about shape shifters—Skinwalkers—and that the locals believed a few things of their own. But then again, almost all the locals were Native American and there were a few hundred more living on the reservation.

"So you're telling me these tracks were made by a Skinwalker?"

He shrugged and gestured with a nod of his head in the direction of the creek. "The people who live there on the other side say that this thing came straight up to their house. Scared the shit out of their animals; that they all fled to the far side of the corral as if trying to get as far away as they could.

"The guy who owns the place, he was in his house, said he heard some kind of commotion, some kind of howl or scream and he and his kid came running out into the yard. It was towards evening, but not yet dark. They said the first thing that hit them was this overwhelming stench of rotting meat, like something had died and gone ripe. And they swore that smell was not there before. There was no way they'd miss that. It was that bad. So bad that there was no way they were going any further into the yard. And just as the guy was pulling his kid back towards to door of the house, they both saw this thing, this creature. It paid no attention to them. Walked on two legs across their path, no more than a hundred feet away, and then, just as it neared the line of trees at the edge of the property, it dropped down to all fours and loped through the trees and down towards the creek, towards where we are standing now; only I'd say it was further down that way." He pointed west.

I admit I was skeptical. "So what did this thing look like? Are we talking Jack Nicholson?" He looked at me like he didn't get the reference. But then again, *Wolf* wasn't one of Jack's best movies. I gave him a quick summary. He said he didn't see it. But he got my meaning.

Lost on Skinwalker Ranch

He smirked as if it was his turn with the skepticism. "No one gives much detail. And supposedly lots of people have seen this thing, or at least something like it. Sometimes it's called a dog-man. Others describe it as a mangy coyote or wolf. It's always hairy and skinny, as tall as the average man and walking on two legs. Some say it has like kangaroo arms, kind of short and held up out front. But it always has canine features for the head and face: pointed ears, the dog-type nose and muzzle and the eyes. And even standing upright, it has a canine-like chest and knees—if dogs have knees."

He told me more of the stories he had heard as we made our way back in the direction of the pastures. We came to the area of the road where it was less rock and more field and started to cut across in the direction of the dog runs. The ground was completely blanketed with about five inches of snow, none of it disturbed.

As we got to a place where we had a clear view of it, Mark pointed out to the ridge and said, "They call that Skinwalker Ridge. Some say it's the path of the Skinwalker and that the Skinwalker's back in those canyons. It's been there since when all of this belonged to the Indians."

It may have been the power of suggestion, but that night when we went out to do the patrol things got a weird. Mark took the East Gate and I went up on the mesa. We only patrolled the part from the corral over towards the gate. Everything west of the corral belonged to this guy Hickens.

The trail up the mesa, which I've already mentioned, is probably as long as a football field, maybe a bit more, and climbs on an angle across the face of the ridge, not straight up. The terrain is rocky, but firm enough that as long as you're careful and look out for loose soil, there's no worry of losing your footing. Still, it takes some athletic walking and is a hell of a workout. I was a little out of breath when I got up there.

Lost on Skinwalker Ranch

I couldn't have been on level ground for more than a couple of minutes when I thought I was hearing drums. My first thought was a radio, maybe a car somewhere nearby, the way sound carries around here. But the drums were not the kind you'd associate with radio music. They were more the tom-tom kind, the kind you associate with Indians, with a real simple beat. The sound was strong and steady and coming from east of my position. I started walking towards it and at the same time thumbed my walkie-talkie. There was some crackle and it took a couple of tries to reach Mark. I asked him if he was hearing what I was hearing. He said no.

The beat was steady and audible: Boom-boom, boom-boom. I clicked him again and told him where I thought it was coming from. But he again said he wasn't hearing anything.

I continued to walk in the direction of the drumming, picturing some old Indian from the reservation sitting cross-legged and reliving the old days. But as if something was fucking with my head, as I thought I was getting closer, the sound was getting lower; but not as if the drums were moving away from me. It was more like someone was watching me and as I drew nearer with each stride, they lowered the volume little by little. Then suddenly it just stopped. I too stopped walking and listened. And then, as if it was a stereo with A and B speakers, the drums started up again, but back in the direction from which I had come in the first place.

There was no way there were two old Indians up here.

I hit up Mark again on the walkie-talkie and told him to meet me at the top of the trail. I told him that I was definitely hearing drums and that I wanted him to get up here so that he could tell me if I was hearing things or not. He didn't blow me off. He believed what I was saying.

Needless to say, when he arrived, the drumming had stopped altogether. I made it to the trail before him—he had a lot further to go and then he had to make the climb—and I was hearing the drums

Lost on Skinwalker Ranch

all the way, until I got there. So I was sure, if he was anywhere close, that he would have heard them too.

After he told me 'no' for like the sixth time, he said, "Shit like this happens all the time. You're not the first guy to say he saw or heard something. Bob—I don't know if you know him—he swears he hears this girl talking to him. Supposedly she died here on the ranch or was killed here back when the whites were settling in the area, and now she haunts the place. But then again, Bob's a little above it all."

I didn't get the drift and I guess he could see it on my face even in the pale halo of the flashlights. You have to keep in mind how dark it was out here. Occasionally, you see lights off in the distance, but there just specks. They don't light anything up.

"You'll know once you get the chance to work with him. He'll be giving you orders and shit."

We called it a night not too long after that. The snow had started to fall again and it seemed there was a rather sudden drop in the temperature.

As we got to the trailer, Mark said, "Make sure to put the drums in your report. The home office loves that kind of stuff. Give them lots of detail."

Lost on Skinwalker Ranch

5: Outside My Window

When I say that I have this particular recurring dream, I don't mean it's a routine. It's not like it's on a schedule. Let me put it this way: I have it enough to call in recurring, but not enough to say it's monthly or even once every two or three months. It happens when it happens, and when it does happen, I can't say it's the same figure or person or whatever you want to call it.

Like I said, it's not as if I recall anything all that specific, other than it looms over the end of the bed; not hovering in the air like a ghost, but has its feet on the ground—the way you'd expect a real person to. Sometimes I'm thinking it's someone who broke into my house and at others, like it's some sort of ghost or spirit who is curious or belongs there. Maybe they lived there in the past before the house was built. Think Poltergeist. I even swore the one time that it was my grandfather, and he's been dead I don't know how many years now. What do I know? These are the kinds of thoughts you have when you're trying to make sense of things that don't make sense.

But there on the ranch, after that first night when Mark heard me yell out, I was having a visitor like every night. By that time, we had a routine going. We would do the night patrol, come back usually around 2:00, more or less—depending on the weather or if something was going on—which didn't happen much, sit around, watch TV and bullshit; and I always had my two fingers. Mark passed as often as he took part. To each his own; it kept the supply from dwindling too quickly. I also tended to turn in before he did. He made the point that he was good with four or five hours of sleep and a nap in the afternoon, which he took religiously. It wasn't my thing, but I could see how it could become a habit, especially out here in the middle of nowhere.

Lost on Skinwalker Ranch

About the fourth time that it happened, which was the beginning of my second week there, I asked Mark if he heard anything coming from my room. He shook his head and asked why. I told him I had the dream again.

Being an ex-cop himself—I think he said he made detective, he asked for the details. There wasn't much I could tell him, other than I was sure it was the same visitor as the nights before. But I did tell him the whole thing was kind of wearing thin on me. He asked what I thought about setting up the video camera that night to see if we could catch anything. It wouldn't be anything sophisticated. There was a tripod. We'd set the thing up from the far corner of the room, the wall with the window, point it at the foot of the bed and turn it on.

So that's what we did.

Of course, knowing that the camera was there and running—I want to say filming, but we don't use film any more—I found it difficult to fall asleep. But thanks in part to the Jack Daniels, it came of its own accord. That last time I checked, the LCD display from the clock on the nightstand beside my bed showed it was 3:17. I don't remember checking again after that.

Here's what I do recall.

I was lying on my back, my head centered in the pillow. The sheet and blanket were pulled up to my chin. I don't remember having anything like a feeling I was being watched. I simply opened up my eyes, for whatever reason, and this tall, wide-shouldered figure was standing at the end of the bed. I know in the way that you know these things when dreaming that it was staring at me, but I can't tell you a single feature, not the eyes or the shape of the face, none of that. But I know I was looking into those eyes and that the face had features. I couldn't help but feel that it wanted to do me harm, to knock me unconscious or brain me completely.

It was only a matter of seconds, of tenths of seconds, and then my feet, fired by a sudden surge of adrenalin, kicked out, but uselessly, restricted by the covers. At the same time, I bolted upright in bed and

Lost on Skinwalker Ranch

had my fists punching out with all my strength at the empty darkness before me. I was still deep into the dream with this happening. It was the violent thrashing out that woke me up. With my eyes now fully open, my heart was beating so hard I was actually nauseous and the fingers on my right hand were tingling from hyperextending my elbow so forcefully.

I sat there upright for a number of minutes, afraid to move that the additional exertion would cause my heart to explode. My eyes moving about the darkness, the light coming from beneath the door enough to make out the shape of the dresser and such, I searched for anything that would suggest there was an actual presence in the room with me. But, of course, there was nothing. I could see by the light on the camera that it was still recording. I was tempted to see what it caught if anything, but instead got up out of bed to turn it off. It gave me the opportunity to move around a little. It's a trick I've learned to reset my heart beat. Walking brings everything back in tune, as it were.

Before getting back in bed, I listened to see if Mark was still up, assuming that if I had yelled anything—I didn't think I did, he would have heard and come to check. But there were no sounds outside the door, for example the television. He must have gone to bed already. I looked at the clock. It was 4:21. I had been asleep for little more than an hour, which was consistent with my previous episodes. I put my middle finger to my wrist and counted a few beats. I doesn't matter what the number was, only that it was once again beating normally.

Once back in bed, perhaps the cold of the room had something to do with it, I pulled up the covers and snuggled in as deeply as I could, and fell asleep fairly immediately. I know this only because I woke up exactly four hours later from the last time I checked the clock. It was 8:21.

I made bacon and eggs for breakfast that morning, only the second time I had something other than oatmeal. The smell of the bacon woke Mark and he joined me. Normally, he wasn't a breakfast guy,

Lost on Skinwalker Ranch

preferring to go only with his coffee and sometimes orange juice. I don't know how he does it, a guy that big.

While we were eating, I told him that we might have something on the camera. It took him a moment to get my meaning, but then I could see it on his face. It kind of psyched him up. He asked for the details and I told him what I could remember. He wanted to check it out before we went out to do our patrol, so while I went in to the shower, he broke down the camera and set up his laptop. He had the adapter that connected the camera right to the computer.

I had hoped he would wait until I was with him before he looked at the video, but as I came out of the bathroom, rubbing my hair with the towel, he said, "You got to see this."

Just the way he said it started my heart on the uptick. "Let me get a shirt and a pair of socks and I'll be right there."

He was shaking his head slowly side to side. "No hurry. It's not going anywhere."

I noticed he said 'it' and not something more ominous, but I didn't know if I should feel better about that or worse.

I stood behind Mark looking down and past his shoulder at the monitor there on the work table. It took me a second to orient myself to figure out what I was looking at. There was just enough light to make out the outline of my body beneath the blankets, a portion of which were tinted green by the glow of the clock which was just out of frame to the left.

"Watch this! Watch this!" Mark repeated with obvious excitement and clearly anticipating the unfolding scene.

Suddenly, there at the end of the bed, as if appearing out of nowhere, there was this commotion of these small illuminated orbs, all red in color and no bigger than my fist, if even that big. I'm tempted to say they were pulsating, but that's not the right word. Animated might be a better description. Either way, the light they

Lost on Skinwalker Ranch

were emitting wasn't all that intense, but it was definitely a light—and not a surface light. It was clearly showing from the inside out.

Unlike the orbs captured on the photos, these definitely had more noticeable depth and shape. You could see they were three dimensional. Altogether, I counted eight, maybe ten of them; it was hard to be sure. They would fade in random order and without pattern, the light extinguished completely, only to be replaced by another or, perhaps, it was the same ones reappearing in a different location. Nevertheless, they remained in motion there at the end of the bed and no others appeared anywhere else in the room from what we could see.

I made some sort of sound of disbelief to which Mark said, "Wait, you ain't seen nothing yet."

I watched for a few more seconds as the orbs continued to do their thing. Then as soon as they came, they were gone, and in their place, though it took a couple of seconds for me to notice, there was this amorphous shape visible only by a deeper darkness against the dark of the room. There was no denying that it had the form of a man, or at least a man-like being, and was as conceivably tall and as wide. Even shaped only by an absence of light, you could see where the head was and the torso and the extremities. It was animated and moving, if not very much, almost as if unsure of its purpose.

Then, the very next instant, you can see a quick abrupt jerk of the covers there at the end of the bed. In the blink of an eye, the red orbs return and then just as suddenly, they swirl together, shift to the left and are gone out of frame. And there I am, sitting straight up and punching out at the darkness.

I caught myself staring dumbfounded at the monitor, and when I finally did say something, I think it was, "What the fuck was that?"

Mark for the most part ignored my reaction, and instead said, "So, did you see what I saw?"

I assumed he meant something besides the obvious. "Is there something you saw that I didn't?"

Lost on Skinwalker Ranch

"Watch, I'll play it again—the part I want you to see. If you look, and at first it's not noticeable given the angle of the camera, but if you look at where the black mass is, the figure, you'll see that you can't see through it. You can't see you in the bed. But if you look where the camera is not blocked, you can see where you are, or at least your shape beneath the covers."

It was freaky, but when he showed it to me again and I knew what to look for, he was right. Whatever it was, was actually there in the room. It was physical and it was real.

Right then and there we looked at each other, and almost as one, we headed for my room. What we were looking for, I can't say with any certainty. But we didn't find anything either, not in the room anyway. However, Mark had the idea to check by the window since that was the direction in which the orbs moved when they went out of frame. The window itself was locked, not for any other reason than it was winter and cold and therefore no reason to open it, and the outside glass was frosted up pretty good. There was also some condensation on the inside from the heat being on. Mark used the side of his hand to wipe away the moisture so he could get a better look outside. What he saw was enough for him to open up the window.

He stepped aside and motioned me over. "Come get a look at this."

It hadn't snowed again since the other day, and with the cold, what snow there was had become ice encrusted on the surface and really powdery beneath. There in the snow outside the window was a clear set of tracks leading away. Everything else around it was undisturbed surface. From where we stood, the tracks looked like little more than elongated imprints down into the snow. There was no discernable shape.

So that's where we started our patrol. But even outside and kneeling down right beside them, we couldn't say with any certainty

Lost on Skinwalker Ranch

they were the same tracks we had seen down by the creek those few days back. The snow was just too powdery to hold any form.

We did track them south to the gulch and even made the descent down towards the creek's edge. The tracks led right to the water—which of course was frozen solid—but there was no indication of tracks on the other side. That whatever it was that made the tracks went on to the ice was obvious. After that, your guess is as good as mine.

"You want to cross over and take a look?" I asked.

Mark shook his head. "You can see from here there's no tracks, not straight across. It is possible that it stayed to the ice and went either east or west." He then suggested we each take a direction.

I went west, but I had no intention of going all that far. Regardless, as careful as I was, stopping every few yards or so to make sure I didn't miss anything, I found only one sign of prints and they were definitely deer. I found them first on this side and saw that they continued right in line on the other, crossing at a point where the ground was fairly level.

Mark didn't find anything of interest either. After that we resumed our normal routine, first walking over to the South Gate, then cutting across the scrub towards the pasture between the second and third dog run and up to the west road. It was business as usual.

Lost on Skinwalker Ranch

6: Rare Currency

Joan dropped me off at the Vernal Regional Airport for an early flight that Sunday, the official end for my first two week shift. Mark came along for the ride to pick up some things he needed. Options are limited in the stores in Roosevelt and Fort Duchesne—not that Vernal is any great mecca, either. That Friday, he had rescheduled his flight so that he could do the company a favor and stay a couple of extra days. Apparently, it was something he did routinely when there were scheduling conflicts. Two other guys were expected to rotate in that coming Wednesday morning. As for me staying, I wasn't asked. And I'm glad. I needed to get away and clear my head. Although I hadn't been bothered by the dream after the filming episode, I found it difficult to fall asleep and would lay awake thinking I was hearing shit and opening my eyes at the slightest sound.

Once the plane touched down at McCarran, I retrieved my bags and grabbed a cab back to my place at my parents'. It's not much of a ride distance-wise, just a few minutes south-west. The house is not the one I grew up in. They sold that after I graduated high school and went out of state to college, down to Texas. I won't say which school. But it was D-1 and I did receive a full sport scholarship. Anyway, I was the last of four kids, so they found a smaller place further north but still comfortably south of Las Vegas. My two brothers and my sister, all older, the youngest of the three by five years, all live out of state.

The house is a two story ranch with a separate apartment upstairs. It was that way when they bought the place—everything legal. There's an outside set of stairs that climbs up along the side of the house where the garage is and meets up with a pretty nice deck that looks out over the backyard. The entrance is a pair of sliding glass doors that open up into the kitchen. There's a living room beyond that, at

Lost on Skinwalker Ranch

the front of the house. My bedroom, which has an on suite bath, is also along the back of the house and there's a second bedroom which serves as an office and a second, smaller half-bathroom with a shower. They're also to the front. There's internet service and I have a dish network for watching television. There's a double driveway leading up to the garage. I park on the far side and Mom and Dad park one behind the other on the side closest to the front door. The garage itself is used for storage, but is fairly empty.

After unpacking my things, I went down the stairs and around to the back of the house where there was a matching set of sliding glass doors. My mother, recently turned 70, spent most of her time in the kitchen and the doors were always unlocked. She and my dad were having lunch. We spent a few minutes catching up on two weeks of news and me answering their questions about being in Utah. I left out the part about the dreams, but shared a little about some of the other stuff. I then left to run a couple of errands. My refrigerator was empty and I wanted to gas up the car and give it a run. I had given the keys to my dad and told him to use it now and then when he had some place to go. He took them and hung them on a hook beside the pantry, asking "Where do I go?" So I'm sure the car hadn't been started since I left.

There's this local bar not too far from the house that my dad and I often go to on Sundays to watch football, especially the late afternoon games. We bullshit with the regulars, have a few beers and chicken wings, yell at the television, regardless of whether play is good or bad, and take our leave with a nice buzz, but always where at least one of us is in shape to drive—usually my father. I've never seen a guy make a beer last so long. That said, I can't recall the last time I was in there by myself, if ever.

Nevertheless, having completed my errands, I had this urge to stop in and have a cold beer, promising myself as I walked through the door it'd only be one. Besides, I had some groceries in the trunk of

Lost on Skinwalker Ranch

the car that I didn't want to defrost, which despite temperatures only in the 40s, they most probably would if I hung around too long.

Now this is where things go weird.

No sooner had I sat down and Ringo, the bartender—it's his place, had brought me a frosted mug of tap beer—it was always fresh and crisp in this place, this guy pulled up the stool next to me and sat down. I swear he came out of nowhere. At least I didn't notice him when I came in. I saw only two other guys, both seated at the far end of the bar, and they hadn't moved. And I'd swear he didn't come in the door behind me. I would have noticed. Ringo, who was pouring a refill for one of those other guys, looked up twice as if he too had just become aware of another customer. "I'll be right with you," he said, going back to his pour.

I took a quick look at the guy, catching mostly his profile. He was definitely Indian, which around these parts isn't uncommon. There's a huge Paiute Reservation just west of 215, and another twenty or so, Navajo and others, sprinkled throughout the state. As for what he looked like, his hair was black, pulled tight and braided down his back well past his shoulder blades. In the low light of the bar, and although he wasn't yet looking at me, I could see that his face was leathery and weather worn. Like most Indians—I don't mean to stereotype, he had no obvious facial hair. Despite the cold, he wore no coat, only a faded flannel shirt which was just this side of thread bare around the collar and the elbows—at least the one closest to me. It was different shades of red with some navy blue. I didn't see it right away, but after we got to talking, I noticed the buttons were bigger than most, brass by their appearance, and joined by eye-hooks of some sort instead of the usual button holes. It was an old-fashioned look. He had on a pair of jeans in no better condition than the shirt and not any brand I'd recognize. They were held in place by a plain leather belt, sort of deerskin in color, and with an oversized buckle that looked to be of iron or something equally as heavy and solid. His boots were black leather,

Lost on Skinwalker Ranch

creased and lined with age and with some major scuff marks along the pointed toes.

When Ringo came over, the guy asked for "Old No. 7". It caught my attention; I don't think I've ever heard of it called anything but Jack or Jack Daniels.

As Ringo was getting him a glass and going for the bottle, the guy took a fold of bills from his pant pocket, pealed one off and placed it on the bar in front of him. I didn't look to see the denomination. Ringo poured the glass, no ice, and swept up the bill. He turned towards the register, stopped in his tracks and turned back. "You sure you want me to cash this?" I could hear in his tone there was something about the bill that wasn't every day.

The guy seemed not to get the gist of the question. He started to go back into his pocket. "Not enough?"

Ringo placed the bill down on the bar in front of him. "It's one of those silver certificates. Looks pretty old to me."

The guy shrugged and said, "It looks like five dollars to me."

Ringo gave me a glance and then went back to the Indian. "Do you mind?" he asked, and meeting no resistance, slid the bill over to me.

It was an absolutely beautiful bill with blue serial numbers and a red stamp on the bottom and just left of center. Up in the right hand corner there was a capital V and beneath it the date 1886. The picture of Ulysses S. Grant was to the right and a number five to the left. Between the two, it said Five Silver Dollars payable to the bearer on demand. The image of the Morgan silver dollar was on the back. Overall, the bill was showing some wear, but the color was good, especially the brighter green on the reverse side. I had no idea at the time what its value was, but I was confident it was much more than five dollars.

I slid it back over to the guy. "You really should keep that one."

He had the folded bills in his hand. "I don't think it's all that much different than what I have here."

Lost on Skinwalker Ranch

He proceeded to unfold the bills and fan them out with his thumb. I can't say I saw every inch of every bill, but from what I did see, every one of them were silver certificates. He then said to Ringo, "If the money's good, take it and do with it what you will."

So that's what he did and he put three singles down in its place. I did notice, though, that he placed the $5 beneath the register tray.

I checked later that night on EBay to see what those things were worth, and depending on condition, bills that old can go for thousands of dollars. Ringo must have had some idea because he didn't take another dollar from that guy while I was there.

But the bills were only the beginning of it, at least as far as I was concerned.

I went back to my beer. There was a no-name bowl game starting so most of my attention was on the TV which was up at my end of the bar. And remember, I had no intention of staying. As soon as my beer was done, I was out of there.

Between sips of beer, I noticed this kind of stale smell. I don't know how to describe it, other than distracting. If I had to compare it something, I'd say it was sort of a wet dog smell, but maybe worse—more like that smell you get on your hands when you pet an old dog whose hair isn't what it used to be. If you've smelled that smell before, you know what I'm talking about. I was sure it was coming from the Indian.

I kind of turned towards him without seeming like I was turning towards him so that I could get a better whiff. Of course, just at the same time, he turned towards me. It was like when you're driving along on the highway and you just happen to look out the passenger side window and the guy driving alongside you looks at the same time. You get the awkward moment, and you either turn away quickly or nod. Well, I nodded.

He responded by getting Ringo's attention and ordering a refill for himself and me, and the rest of the house besides. I was all set to beg

Lost on Skinwalker Ranch

off, but it didn't seem right insulting the guy, him being an Indian and all. He peeled off another bill, but Ringo wouldn't take it.

I went for a shot of the Jack.

Together we toasted our benefactor and down the hatch it went.

At that point, having taken a drink from the guy, it was only polite that I acknowledge him, so I introduced myself, giving him my first name.

He responded by telling me his name was Curtis Sammer.

I thought he said 'summer'. But when I attached a mister to it during our conversation, he corrected me—it sounded like 'hammer'—and said to make it Curtis.

Then what started off as the usual small talk suddenly took a turn towards the unexpected.

"If I said I had a proposition that could be profitable to the two of us, would you be interested?"

By this time we were on a second shot of Jack—Ringo took my money—and I hadn't yet made up my mind about the guy. There was something about him I couldn't put my finger on. Usually, I can look into a person's eyes and get a pretty good read. But not this guy. His eyes were odd. First of all, they had to be the darkest I had ever seen, nearly coal black, but deep and clear. The whites of his eyes, however, were just the opposite. They were yellow like the eyes, well, of old people. And he wouldn't make direct eye contact when talking with me, either looking over at the TV or at the bottles along the top of the bar. As for the way he talked, his voice had this distinct inflection and he had a funny way of putting his words together. Though it was nothing like it, really, he made me think of Yoda. If you asked me to give him an age, I would say early 60s. But the truth is, he seemed so out of time and place that he could have been much older.

But back to his proposition. Going with the flow, I said, "I guess that would depend on the proposition." If never crossed my mind the guy was gay or anything like that.

Lost on Skinwalker Ranch

That's when he reaches into the breast pocket on the left side of his shirt and takes out a coin which he then hands to me. "What do you think that is worth?"

I took the coin and seeing the way it was tarnished, I knew immediately it was silver. I thought at first it was a Morgan, but flipping it over a couple of times, I could see that it wasn't from the United States. It had the name Carlos III—I don't remember exactly—on the face and the words Hispan and Rex on the back. It was dated 1804.

"It's Mexican," he said. "An ocho reales piece."

I handed it back to him. "It's nice."

"Its value?"

I had no idea and said as much. "You'd have to take it to a coin dealer. I would think the silver content alone is probably between $15-20. A collector, though, would pay a lot more."

"What if I told you I know where there's many more of these? And not only these, but different ones, some of solid gold?"

I had to admit he had me intrigued, but I was also feeling more than a little skeptical, even suspicious. "I'd say why tell me?"

"A stranger, you mean."

I nodded.

He looked to see, I presume, where Ringo was—he was down the other end talking—and then making no effort to lower his voice or anything, he said, pausing a moment, "Let's say you wanted to have your wife done away with, but didn't want to do it yourself. Would you ask your brother or an acquaintance to do it, or would you, perhaps, look to a stranger?"

I couldn't help but wonder if he was making an accusation or fishing for something. But I got a hold of myself. First of all, he didn't know me and wouldn't know the wife and I were separated; and second, I had no intention of knocking her off. "I guess I would go with the stranger."

Lost on Skinwalker Ranch

"Of course you would. As would I. This proposition is no different. As what I am after will take some risk, I would prefer someone who can do the job, and once done, will go his own way as I will go mine. And as we know nothing significant of each other, was either one of us to attract the attention of the authorities, the other has nothing to worry about."

"I'll take it your name isn't really Curtis Sammer?"

He had no visible reaction whatsoever. "The name is real enough," he shrugged.

Fair enough, I thought, and went on with the game. "So, where is this buried treasure?"

He looked down at his empty glass. "Never said it was buried." Then he paused and not looking up, he said, "It is a place called Indian Canyon, on a reservation. There's a string of caves along a hidden ridge that very few know. Nonetheless, the area in general is watched closely by the Bureau of Land Management and reservation police."

I felt he was being evasive. "There's a lot of reservations around here and lots of canyons."

This time our eyes met, if only for a second, and I couldn't help but notice how feral they suddenly looked, even if it was only the way the light hit them there in the pale of the bar. "It's in Utah, inside the Uintah-Ouray Reservation. Not too far outside a Native town called Fort Duchesne."

My first impression was that he was playing with me, that he had to know, somehow, that I had just come from there.

He must have read the expression on my face. "You know it?"

I lied. "Never been there."

He showed no reaction and instead said, "I'll be back there in a fortnight—fifteen days to be exact. I have some things to take care of first."

This was nearly too much. I was scheduled to go back there in two weeks to do my second shift at the ranch. But again, there was no

Lost on Skinwalker Ranch

way he could know that. It all had to be coincidence: the comment about my wife, the location and the time.

I felt like I needed to get away from him for a moment, so I slid off the stool and excused myself to the men's room. As I walked towards the far corner to the back of the bar I was tempted to look back to see if he was watching—but I didn't.

When I came back out, he wasn't where I had left him. I gave a look around, but didn't see him. So unless he was in the ladies room, which I doubted, he must have left.

I went back to where I was sitting and Ringo was there wiping down the bar.

"What happened to Tonto?" I asked.

Ringo gave a little shrug. "He told me to tell you he'd be back in touch." He gestured to my empty glass with a flip of his bar towel. "He left that."

There by the glass was the silver coin, the piece of eight.

My first thought was to leave it with Ringo as a tip. But then I thought, what the heck, it just may be worth something. I put it in my pocket, said good day and left a few singles on the bar instead.

I didn't realize until I got into my car that my watch had stopped. What happened was that when I started the car, I saw the time on the dash and couldn't believe that it was almost 4:00. I had been in the bar for near on three hours. So naturally, I checked my watch—it's the kind with hands—and it showed that it was only a few minutes after one—but the second hand was definitely moving. It must have just started ticking again on its own.

7: Someone's At the Door

I had to go to work at BAASS' Las Vegas property on Monday. So after I got back home, I put away my groceries and popped in on my folks to have something to eat. My mother always cooked Italian on Sundays and drinking made me hungry. After the meal, I hung out about another hour to have a cup of coffee, which I needed, and slice of cake my mother had baked. I then said good-night and went up to my apartment to watch some TV. Since I had to be at work by 8:00 a.m., and I was feeling the drag of the travel and the effects of more to drink than I had intended, I went into bed before 10:00.

As far as I know, I feel asleep about as soon as my head hit the pillow. And this time, unlike my stay on the ranch, it was no dream that awakened me. Instead, there was an overwhelming and very palpable feeling that someone was there in the house with me.

I lay on my left side, the open door of my bedroom to my back and to the right. Whatever or whoever it was made no sound, nor was there any indication of movement. My heart pounding in my chest and the adrenalin sharpening my senses, I considered my options. My first thought was to remain as still as possible in the hope that if thought to be sleeping, whoever was here would be less likely to do anything rash.

Even in that little pocket of time, my brain was working through the possibilities. I settled on the idea of a burglar, some guy climbing the stairs to the deck and shimmying open the sliding glass doors. Why not? The backyard is dark. The back of the house is dark. It's an easy in. Search a few drawers. Grab some electronics, the wallet. Out you go.

My plan was to go for the 9mm in the draw of the night table. But it was also to my back, and if my visitor was watching me, one of two things would then happen. I'd be rushed or he'd make a break for the

Lost on Skinwalker Ranch

back door. I decided to go for it; human nature, in a situation like that, is to run. People that break into houses are looking for an easy mark, not a confrontation.

So I did.

I spun beneath the blanket and reached for the drawer with my left hand. Being right handed, it wasn't what I would have preferred, but my options were limited. The draw came right open; my hand immediately found the grip of the gun. I sat up and at the same time switched the pistol to my right hand and took off the safety. I've had lots of practice.

"Get the fuck out of here or I'm going to blow your brains out," I barked menacingly at the darkness. It came out louder than I had intended, but definitely sounded convincing enough.

I expected to hear footsteps, maybe some shit crashing as the intruder made for the kitchen. But there was nothing.

I sat there for a few seconds—seemed like a lot longer—before I decided to reach for the switch on the lamp. I gave it a push with my thumb and the light flared. Everything was quiet and still.

I threw the covers off the rest of the way and swung my feet to the floor. Unable to fully shake the feeling of some presence, I stood and approached the door in slow, noiseless steps, trying not to give my exact position away.

The truth is I doubted there was anyone standing there in the dark outside my room. It would take some set of balls to hang around after being threatened by some guy with a gun and in his own house. Logic tells you, the investment isn't worth getting shot.

But even so, there was an anxiety that I couldn't quite shake. I mean, and I hate to admit it, I think I was scared, scared that there was something looming right at the edge of the darkness.

There's a light switch beside the door. I approached it out of direct line to the opening and flicked it up. The fixtures, all recessed, lighted up every corner of the room and flooded out across the hallway floor and to the opposite wall.

Lost on Skinwalker Ranch

Now, I realize this is going to sound like bullshit, but I swear there was a mass of darkness that held its shape against the glow of the light, if only for a fraction of a second, before it seemingly stepped backwards and was gone. With it went the feel of anxiety in the pit of my stomach and I suddenly felt very foolish, hoping that my parents weren't awakened by my yelling and cursing and I'd have to come up with some explanation.

Just to satisfy my curiosity and to make certain it was all in my mind, I walked into my kitchen and gave the door handles a tug. They were securely locked.

As long as I was up, I got myself a cold glass of water—I have one of those refrigerators that provide both water and ice—and then went in to take a piss. On my way to the bathroom, I paused to give the living room a once over and then listened for any stirring from the floor below. There was nothing.

Surprisingly enough, I was feeling pretty relaxed, and as it was only a little after midnight, I saw no reason to not get back into bed and finish off a good night's sleep. To give myself peace of mind, I checked the pistol to make sure the safety was on and slipped it beneath my pillow.

I knew nothing more about the world until the alarm went off.

Work that day, and every day after, was pretty routine. It was my second time around there at BAASS, so I had a good idea as what to expect. For the most part, I did foot patrol both inside and outside the facility making sure that everything was as it was supposed to be.

My partner those two weeks was the guy Bob that Mark had told me about. My first impression was that he was a bit full of himself, but other than that he was pleasant enough and the kind of guy that grows on you. He was really impressed by the ranch, and although we were discouraged from talking about the place, even to each other, he seemed not to hold himself to that particular expectation. We had

Lost on Skinwalker Ranch

some pretty good conversation, especially as we spent time together and his trust in me grew—at least, that's how I saw it.

It was his opinion that the ranch was haunted—my word, not his—by both good and malevolent spirits. He didn't say evil. It was his thing that they weren't demons or devil-like, but more so, by nature, unpleasant. He said that if you left yourself open, the less friendly ones would find a way in over the good.

I didn't know what he meant by that, but he sounded convinced that he knew the difference between the two. He even went so far as to say he could summon the good ones and evict the evil ones. That was the word he used—evict. He said he could tell the difference by the size and color of the orbs, and that there was a distinct and unmistakable sense of dread whenever the ill-humored ones were around.

His favorite story was about this girl. He said she was probably around thirteen years old or so and was killed there on the ranch, supposedly out by the old homestead. He had no details and couldn't say if he thought she had died there more recently or way back in the past, but that he had little doubt she was a victim and herself not malevolent. He said he sensed she had blonde hair, so I'll go with the assumption that she wasn't an Indian.

My understanding is that if you go back to the last two owners, which covers at least from the 50s, neither one of them had a daughter that age. The first ones, the Meyers, didn't have any children at all from what I was told, at least not while they were living there. As for the Shermans, the family that bought it from old lady Meyers after the husband passed, they had two kids. One was definitely a girl, but she's still well and living—as is the son, and again, as far as I know, neither one ever came to any physical harm while the family stayed there.

But back to Bob's story: When I asked him how he knew the girl was present, he talked about hearing her laughter. He said their first encounter was out by the old homestead. He and this other security

Lost on Skinwalker Ranch

guy, Nick, had heard the story and decided they'd try to contact her. At first, all they were getting were the usual photos of orbs. That's when he came up with the idea of trying to contact her telepathically using some information he read in a book he took out of his local library after he started working at the ranch.

The way he tells it, he just started visualizing her in his head and her appearing. He then started saying shit aloud, basically telling the girl he knew she was there and asking her to give some kind of sign that she understood. "Well," he said, every bit of awe in his tone, "we had Rucca with us. She was just sitting there and then starts getting excited, letting out this high pitched, yet really quiet whining. You know, yipping and giving us the look. I had hold of the leash, since Nick was taking photos. She gets up but can't seem to make up her mind what she wants to do. One moment she's walking away from me and towards the homestead, the next she's retreating and kind of hiding behind my legs.

"Now, Nick and I are standing on the dirt road, the path that's there, and he's pointing to the homestead. The stupid dog is still doing what it was doing, and I look to where Nick's pointing, and there's this orb. One of the biggest ones we've seen, and it's no photo. It's the real thing. It was a light orange in color, pretty much transparent, but definitely a sphere in shape. And it's not like we could see through it."

At this point, I'm thinking all kinds of skeptical questions I can ask or comments that I can make, but seeing how intense he is telling it, I let him keep going.

"Anyway, it is about, I don't know, four feet, maybe a little more, off the ground; suspended there and not doing anything. I'm not going to say it was glowing, or flashing or fiery, or anything like that. But it did have an aura about it, a light of its own.

"So I let go of Rucca's leash to see if she'd do anything. I didn't know if she'd attack or run in the other direction. But instead, she moves away from me in direction of the orb, only a few feet, kind of

Lost on Skinwalker Ranch

to the edge of the road, but not off of it, and then she lies down in the dirt and rolls over on her back as if wanting a belly rub. And that's the first time I heard the laughter. Then the orb starts to drift at like a walking pace across the front of the homestead, moving away from us and towards the back of the house. And then it ducked around the corner and was gone. The laughter, like a fading echo, went with it."

I wanted to know what the Labrador did. He said she got back to her feet and stood there looking in the direction of the old house but didn't move. So he grabbed her leash before she realized no one was holding her and took off to chase after porcupines.

By the end of that second week, this thing, this presence—whatever it was—had become a real nuisance. It was there every night when I went into bed, there in the darkness outside my room. The sense of its presence became so prevalent that I started leaving the light on in the hallway and sleeping with the door partially closed.

The problem was I wasn't getting much sleep. Every time I managed to nod off and get into that deep sleep that you recognize only when you come out of it, the kind that you need to feel refreshed the next day, to have energy, I would wake with a sudden start. Sometimes it was because of a sound, like a knock or a bang. Sometimes, I thought I saw something, a shadow or a face, there in the room or looming over me, only to awake and realize I was sleeping. On the latest occasion, I swore I felt a hand—just the fingers—slowly and lightly tracing down the inside of my right thigh beneath the covers, from crotch to knee. There was no mistaken how real it was. But again, bolting straight up, which sent my heart pounding, I realized I had been sleeping and there was nothing there to suggest it was anything but in my head.

Needless to say, it was starting to wear on me. Not only was I waking more tired than I felt when I went to bed in the first place, but it was starting to show at work and in my interaction with the people

Lost on Skinwalker Ranch

around me. My concentration wasn't good and I'd often find myself drifting when others were talking to me.

As for weird shit at the house, the last event was probably two days before I was scheduled to go back to the ranch. I was down my parents' way and we were having breakfast. Mom was into the bacon, eggs and pancake thing, so it had to be that Saturday. She was more a fresh bagels and coffee person come Sundays.

Regardless, we were all at the table there in the kitchen, my dad and I talking the usual shit, when my mother, without a word, pushed away from the table, left her plate behind and walked out towards the living room. A few seconds later we heard the front door open. My dad and I just looked at each other and shrugged.

When she came back to the kitchen, my father gave her one of those looks that people who have been married a long time have for each other depending upon the situation.

"I thought I heard someone at the door," she said, her voice trying to hold on to some semblance of certainty.

Dad turned to me without much in the way of an expression and said, "She's being doing that all week."

Mom had a look of her own for him, one that I had seen lots of times before. It's the 'what are you talking about' look. "When?" she said.

"How about yesterday at dinner? We were both sitting right here. How about last night when we were watching the News? Should we mention the other morning while we were having coffee? What was it, Wednesday? Maybe Tuesday?"

Despite the fact that she was telling him he was being silly and imagining things, I had to think there was some truth to it. So I asked if just then she thought she heard knocking, or was it just a feeling that someone was at the door.

She thought about it a second before she answered. "Now that I think about it, I'd say it was a sense, a feeling, almost like a premonition. It wasn't a knock."

Lost on Skinwalker Ranch

"And the other times?"

There was no mistaking her expression. She glanced over at my father as if to see what he was up to, and then back to me. "He put you up to this, didn't he? There weren't any other times." She then laughed as if it was just some sort of prank my father and I had come up with and went back to eating.

My father winked at me and mouthed, "Early dementia." And he too went back to his breakfast.

Going back to the ranch, I was hoping to find some answers.

8: Vanishing Coyotes

I'd been back at the ranch but a couple of days when Joan came knocking on the door of the trailer. It was late morning. Nick and I were taking a look at some video from the night before. We had some visitors outside the South Gate, a dark colored SUV that had pulled up, turned out the headlights and discharged one subject from the rear passenger door. From what we could see, that individual came up to the gate, navigated it successfully and came upon the property. He looked like he used his cellphone to snap a photo or two. He then made a quick exit and the vehicle backed away, going a good distance before the headlights came back on. All in all, it was no big deal but we had to make a formal report any time we had trespassers. It was, however too dark to get the license plate or a clear make of the SUV.

Nick went over to the door and let Joan in. She was always real pleasant with us, and more often than not was dropping by to bring us something she had prepared in the way of a meal, leftovers, that kind of thing. But this time she came empty handed and seemed concerned.

She entered but left her coat on, a sure indication that she had no plans to stay. She had come by to warn us about coyotes. As best as she could figure, or her husband Jack had told her, a band of five or six of them had come up close to the house the night before, and by the looks of the prints they left, right up to the windows and door out back. It had her a bit unsettled. Coyotes on the property were a common occurrence; that they'd come this far up on the property, and to the house itself, well, that was something that hadn't happened before.

Nick and I put our coats on, hats and gloves—it was about ten degrees outside—and let Joan lead us around to the back of her

Lost on Skinwalker Ranch

house. Jack was there already, shotgun in hand, pacing about and taking note of the paw prints running this way and that.

He greeted us with a nod of his head—he wasn't much of a talker—and pointed over to the window outside the kitchen. "Got some prints there that just don't look right," he said.

When I tell you that I couldn't tell one coyote track from another, take my word for it. But that said, I could see that some of these tracks stood out from the others, especially those right around the window.

Nick, who counted himself some sort of an outdoorsman, having, so he says, hunted all kinds of different animals in all kinds of different places, taking obvious care not to trod all over what was there, went down on one knee to get a good look. Talking to me, he said, "See how these here are definitely deeper and longer than these ones over here?" he moved a gloved finger towards the snow to his left. "It's obvious that two of the coyotes were considerably bigger than the others." He again indicated separate sets of tracks moving alongside each other. "Probably older males; some of them can get up to 70 pounds."

Jack, having trailed the tracks a dozen yards or so from the house, turned back and said, "Looks to me like a couple of them were up on their hind legs as if taking a look through the window."

When he said it, I immediately thought to look up on the sill and the vinyl siding. I didn't see anything that looked like paw prints or claw marks. Even a coyote's claws, if not actually scratching, would, I think, at the least, leave some sort of mark. But there was nothing. So I expressed my opinion aloud.

Jack said he was thinking the same thing. "But I've no other explanation for it. You can see how the print elongates at the back, as if the mangy mutts suddenly went flat footed. And then how it gets deeper up by the paws, as if they went up on tiptoe; if you know what I'm getting at."

Lost on Skinwalker Ranch

I had this visual in my head of a couple of coyotes standing upright, front paws held high, muzzles poking back and forth and trying to get a look through the windows.

By this time, Nick had straightened up, made a closer examination of the window and around by the back door—they weren't far apart—and then was striding over to Jack's position. "Looks like they cut back across the open field towards the first dog run. Riley and I will start our patrol in that direction."

Jack said he'd like to go with us, but his back was giving him trouble. "Coyotes are pretty much nocturnal around these parts. But I'd take a gun with me if I were you two."

Nick and I went back to the trailer before officially going out to do the walk. I for one needed to take care of some personal business—we were going to be out in the cold and snow for a couple of hours—and we both wanted to be armed.

Technically, company policy required us to carry a sidearm whenever we were on duty. It was all about professionalism, and it didn't hurt to have a little intimidation factor when face to face with the more daring and nocturnal adventurers tempting to gain access to the property—and I mean the two legged kind. People tend to act stupid after dark, for whatever reason. But keep in mind, our job was security. As necessary, we were directed to detain and then call the local police. We weren't out there to shoot anyone.

We had no intention of hunting the coyotes. If that were so, we would go out with rifles. We were going out with the intent to find out how they got on the property and how they went off. Having the 9mm. was just in case we ran into them. It was all about protection.

We picked up their trail from out back of the ranch house and followed it due west across field one. The band definitely was distracted by the dog run and left prints all along the fence edge as if they were trying to figure out a way in. We assumed they picked up

Lost on Skinwalker Ranch

the scent of our own dogs. Coyotes are known, especially when food is scarce, to attack and eat domestic pets.

After checking the perimeter to make sure they hadn't tried to burrow beneath, which there was no sign of, we stayed with the tracks—easy to follow in the snow—to the tree line separating field one from field two. This is where we noted that the band split into two. Four of the coyotes headed for the trees—I took Nick's word for how many there were—and went south towards the gulch. The two others passed through the opening in the tree line and out into field two towards the second dog run.

We debated splitting up there, but this time Nick agreed picking up the south trail would be easy enough later on. Besides we already knew there were coyotes living in the brush down that way. He wanted to know where the other two were heading, and so did I. If they had a den somewhere on the property, and there were shallow caves and hollows in the ridge north of the road, we wanted to know where. We both had seen and heard coyotes while doing our nightly rounds, but usually they were at a distance. When alone they're not so brave and highly unlikely to attack a human. Not so if they are in packs and hungry.

There was no art to tracking them. We could see as soon as we broke the tree line into field two that the pair was heading straight west across the field and towards field three. That too made sense as there was heavy growth along the western boundary of the property.

About half way across the field, Nick stopped to take a better look at the tracks. It was his opinion, by the size of the prints and the length of the strides, we were tracking the two bigger animals. He suggested they were both males and they seemed to be loping along at a steady pace, but not running.

There's another tree line between field two and three, but unlike the one we passed to get to field two, there's no clearing. The line of trees is unbroken all the way from the road south. But like I said, it's thin, only one, two trees at the most.

Lost on Skinwalker Ranch

We moved through the trees fully expecting the trail to keep going west towards the third dog run, but it didn't. Instead it veered and made a direct line for the copse of trees where homestead two was located.

To make things more difficult, that's like the only spot on the ranch where the road is lined by trees on both sides. From where we stood, it was impossible even through bare branches to see if the coyotes went through the trees and crossed the road towards homestead one, north to the ridge, or if they stayed to the road itself and kept going west.

As we approached the trees around homestead two, Nick and I both became more cautious, taking care where and how we stepped, trying to minimize the sound of crunching snow beneath our heavy boots and beneath the fresher snow there on the surface.

Just out ahead of the first trees, we stopped and Nick signaled with his hand that I stay back while he eyed the trail to get an idea of where it was headed and how far. There's a foot path that leads between the trees where we stood and what remains of homestead two. It's wide enough for the two of us to walk side-by-side. The coyotes' trail led right down the middle. That same path leads into a small clearing which rings the homestead and then around it, both out towards field three and in the direction of the road.

When Nick signaled, I followed, coming up from behind him. Without saying a word, he gestured with a nod of his head to the trail out front. It led right up to the homestead and into the opening where the door used to be before the wood rotted and fell away.

"Looks like they went inside," he whispered.

"So what's your plan?"

"To go check it out."

It was tough to tell if he was serious. He sounded like he was, but as we both wore glasses with polarized lenses, which in the bright reflection of the morning sun were dark and impenetrable, I couldn't see his eyes to be sure.

Lost on Skinwalker Ranch

"You first."

He purposely raised his voice. "This might be the time to start making some noise. Let them know we're here, if they're still in there."

From where I stood, I could only see one clear trail and it went into what was left of the house—sitting length-wise from our perspective—without any indication that the coyotes came back out and went on their way. "They could've gone out a hole in the wall," I supposed, loud enough for Nick to hear me.

Nick nodded. "Probably. If they were still in there, they would have heard us by now, and would have had our scent before that."

That didn't change my stance any, "You first," I repeated.

We both drew our sidearm and clicked off the safety. For anyone watching, we looked like a pair of TV cops, two hands on the gun and arms extended out ahead of us, sidling like snow crabs towards the door. I took up position to the left and let him cross the opening to the right. We stood as still as statues, guns held at the ready, listening for any noise from inside. There was nothing.

Nick looked around at the ground and found a good size branch sticking up out of the snow only a few feet away. By this time, we were trying to make noise, so he kind of stomped over and picked it up. He then came back to the door and still staying off to the side, flicked it with a backhand in through the opening. A second later, we heard it hit the rotted wood of the floor and then again as it bounced. Nothing followed.

We looked at each other and Nick went in, gun still held up and pointing into the home. I went in after him. Since most of the roof is missing, there was plenty of light. Most of the floor, too, is missing, with only the joists still in place in all but the center most section. Here we could make out paw prints in the recent dusting of snow that had filtered down from above. They went straight to the far end where there was a second door and a small space beyond. If they were still here, that's where they'd be—hopefully, sleeping.

Lost on Skinwalker Ranch

I was in no hurry to charge forward, and said, "It would be real stupid of us to go any further. There's nothing that spells disaster like two coyotes feeling trapped in a tiny little space and the only way out through two man-sized steaks. I vote we go outside, around back and see if there's any sign they got out through a hole in the wall."

Nick was in total agreement, so that's what we did.

Only, when we went back outside, we didn't find any sign of any other tracks: not going around the house, not from the front door, and not from any holes in the wall out of which a coyote could have squeezed through if it wanted.

Contrary to what logic told us, this left only one option: the coyotes were still inside. But we knew we had made enough noise to announce our presence, and even if they had been asleep, they don't sleep that deeply. They would have at least growled.

So we went back inside and approached that rear space with some caution. But the truth is, neither one of us expected the coyotes to actually be there. And they weren't. But their prints were, two sets of them, there in the light dusting of snow and almost perfectly formed. It looked like each coyote took one full stride into the middle of the room, which was really no bigger than the average sized closet, and then disappeared, as if beamed up through what was left of the roof.

As I stood there with my lower jaw unhinged, Nick, as if this was something he saw every day, took the camera from out of the backpack he always wore on patrol and began snapping photos. "They're going to love this back at the home office," he said, his head shaking back and forth with disbelief.

Lost on Skinwalker Ranch

9: Awakened

As we walked back to the trailer, my partner visibly anxious to get a message and his photos off to the home office, I couldn't help but press him for what it was he was thinking. I mean, I know what I was thinking, and that was there had to be a logical explanation and we weren't seeing it. There's no way that two coyotes made their way into that building, dilapidated and falling apart as it was, and then out again without leaving tracks. If they made tracks going in. They had to make tracks going out.

"Welcome to the ranch," he said, flashing an 'I told you so' smile—although, up to that point, he hadn't told me anything. "There's all kinds of stories. Do you know the company brought out two investigators, two big shots with all kinds of military and law enforcement experience, to interview the locals?" He paused a moment, but I could tell he wasn't waiting for an answer. "They found out all kinds of weird shit. The Natives—the ones that are stubborn—won't say anything. But the ones off the reservation, they'll tell their stories. And there's the non-natives, too. It's not like whatever is out here limits its activity to Indians only."

He started with "there's this one story…", but I interrupted him, saying he could save the stories for the warmth of the trailer. "Tell me where the tracks went. That's what I want to know."

But he wasn't going to make it that easy on me. "Where do you think they went?"

It sounded stupid, even to me, when I said it out loud. "They went out either the way they came in or found a way through the floor boards and beneath the walls. Could be the wind swept away their tracks or filled them in with blown snow."

The look on his face, polarized lenses or not, told me enough to know how ridiculous he too thought I sounded. "You mean the same wind and snow that couldn't be bothered with the prints we tracked

Lost on Skinwalker Ranch

across the fields. And don't you think at some point they would you have started leaving tracks we could follow? We walked the perimeter around the homestead. Did you see something I didn't?"

Of course I didn't and said as much. "Coyotes are flesh and bone, so there's got to be some explanation that makes sense. It's not like they disappeared into thin air."

He stopped walking which put me a stride ahead of him, so that I had to turn to hear what he had to say. "What if I told you that's exactly what they did?"

"I'd think you were fucking with me."

He nodded. "Okay, and if I told you there's some that think there's a portal by homestead two?"

What was I supposed to say to that? "What do you mean by portal?"

He shrugged and his voice quickened. "A doorway, a passage way, a way to move between dimensions."

I could see he was waiting for me to process his words, and to give me the time, he started walking again. I fell in stride beside him. "Okay, I'll bite. Tell me about dimensions." I hid my skepticism poorly.

He gave me one of those diaphragm chuckles. "What's there to tell? The home office bought this place for a reason. There's some that think this whole area is UFO central. Me, I haven't seen anything alien-like, not the space kind, anyway. But then there's others that think the ranch is sitting in the middle of some kind of alternate dimension highway with these portals that open up between worlds. Again, I haven't seen anything substantial that I can hold up as evidence. But I have seen all kinds of little shit." He hooked his thumb back over his shoulder, "Like disappearing coyote trails and liquid light that trickles down the darkness and fades out in the blink of an eye."

I didn't expect that last one. "Liquid light?"

Lost on Skinwalker Ranch

His lips went thin. "That's what it looks like to me. I've seen it maybe a half-dozen times, and always out that way, between fields two and three and close to the homestead. It's never all that bright and always the same color, a sort of green with purple outline. Always vertical, maybe three or four feet in length and a foot, maybe two off the ground—and narrow." He placed his hands about four inches apart. "You can think of it looking like wax dripping down the side of one of those dinner table candles, the tall, thin cylindrical kind. When it first appears, it has that northern lights look, kind of ghostly; I think the word is ethereal. It lingers for only a moment, a couple of seconds at the best. Then it's gone." He snapped his gloved fingers for effect. There wasn't much in the way of a snap.

I had no doubt that what he was telling me, he was serious. I could hear it in his voice. "You think the light is a portal." I made it a statement.

He responded with a short shrug of his shoulders. "What do I know? It could be some sort of phenomena, some anomaly of light. There's natural gas throughout these rocks. Could be that. Gas escaping. Although I don't know what would make it glow."

I asked him if he saw this light thing in the same place every time. He told me in the same general area, but not the exact same place. But that he had never seen it anywhere else on the ranch, meaning not up on the mesa or down by the gulch.

"And I'll tell you something else," he said as we came across field one and were but a hundred yards from the trailer, "It gives me this shiver in my balls every time I see it, weak in my knees, like it's not natural. Go figure."

The trailer, thankfully, was warm. My fingers and toes needed the thawing; but the rest of me was actually sweating beneath the coat and the layers of clothes. You don't realize how much effort it takes to walk that distance in the snow. Cold or not, your body is burning calories, and burning creates heat.

Lost on Skinwalker Ranch

While we ate a bite for lunch—reheated Hormel chili, Nick put together a report to send off to the Home Office. I basically copied his and put in a few words of my own to provide a personal perspective. We were told that was important, that the people reading these daily logs felt the nuance was necessary. Otherwise, what was the point? They could just as easily assign the reporting to one person.

So as I hadn't seen any liquid lights, I kept to the disappearing paw prints and simply added that I had no explanation as to why they discontinued and then did not continue again. I'd leave the supposition to those who wanted to suppose. Nick had me read his before he sent it off—everything was done via email. He had no concern about mentioning portals, writing, "The coyotes disappeared in the same location as the suspected portal. Will continue to monitor this area."

I had taken to the habit of napping in the late afternoon. Part of it was because there really wasn't much to do between patrol and part of it was because I still wasn't getting the kind of sleep at night that I would have preferred. It wasn't as if I was having the dream every night or the feeling that there was something in the room with me—but there was always something. Sometimes the dreams or visuals, or whatever you want to call them, were so real that I couldn't tell whether I was sleeping or awake—until, of course, I actually awaken and realize that I had been sleeping. Some nights it would come on me only minutes, literally, after falling asleep. Others, it would be three-thirty, maybe four when some weird twist of an otherwise normal dream would cause me to shake myself from my sleep, not wanting to see what was going to happen next.

Last night, for example, was one of the early morning episodes. In the dream, I was in a car and my mother was driving. We were in a blue Maverick. I have no idea how I knew it was a Maverick, but in the dream I just took it for granted. We were going down a side road in town. The road wasn't crowded, or anything like that, but there

Lost on Skinwalker Ranch

were other cars. My mother is driving fast, way too fast for the road, and showing no concern for traffic laws. She's dodging cars to the right, going through stop signs, shit like that. I tell her to slow down. But she insists the grandkids are getting out of school in but a few minutes and she has to pick them up.

Here's the thing: I hadn't been in a car driven by my mother since I was in high school, my dad owned a Ford Maverick in the 70s, and my mother doesn't have any grandchildren still in school.

As the car approaches the intersection with the main road, instead of proceeding along with the other cars—none of which I actually saw, I just knew they were there, she veers hard to the right to cut through a parking lot with an entrance or exit out to the main road going west. The very next moment, I'm no longer in the car, but standing atop a roofless enclosure consisting of three brick walls about six feet tall and with an opening facing east. The enclosure is against the front of a cinderblock building there in the parking lot. I assume it's for keeping the industrial trash container out of sight; but at the moment it's empty.

Just like that, I am inside the enclosure and talking to my sister—she's the sibling closest to my age. I don't remember the conversation, but it has to do with being safe where we were, unless there's gang members, or something along those lines, there in the building and they come out and cut off our escape. And just then, that's exactly what happens. There's two black guys standing in the opening.

The scene shifts: I'm outside the enclosure and physically engaging one of these hoodlums. I hit him three or four times and he's no longer there. Ready to make a run for it, I look back towards the main door of the building and there's this huge, dark figure but a stride from me. It doesn't matter that there's no detail. It was simply menacing and I knew I was fucked.

That's when Nick comes in and tries to shake me awake.

I bolted to an upright position, sitting, and started throwing punches into empty space. But there's light coming in through the

Lost on Skinwalker Ranch

open door. So I'm trying to get my bearings, figure out what's going on. As my eyes are adjusting to the low light levels, out of my peripheral vision I notice movement down on the floor beside the bed. It was Nick seated on his butt, leaning back on the heels of his hands with both legs extended out before him.

"Easy, brother, easy. It's only me," he's saying.

As it turned out, I didn't get him with any of my flailing and punching, but as he leaned back to get out of the way, he slipped on the sneakers that I wear about the trailer. His feet came out from underneath him and he landed on his ass.

Although my heart was still pounding, I had come around to my surroundings. None too happy with the unexpected intrusion, I kind of growled at him. "Well, what the fuck, man—is there something wrong with you? You scared the shit out of me."

Staying where he was down on the floor and keeping his voice low, he said, "I swear, something came in here. I saw it clear as day. There was this shadow right outside your door. I saw it from the kitchen. It lingered for a couple of seconds, and then—I shit you not—it passed right through the closed door as if it wasn't even there. I watched it. Half its body passed through and then the other half followed, just like if you or I walked through an open doorway. Only this door wasn't open, and it wasn't me and it wasn't you.

"I got up and came and stood outside your door listening. I didn't know if I should come in or not. Like it was just my imagination. So I opened the door just enough so I could see in. And as soon as I did, the light from out in the hall, from the kitchen, filtered in, and again I shit you not, the same thing I saw outside your door was there at the end of your bed. I pushed the door open the rest of the way—like it is now—and took a step into the room. But it was as if the light coming in swept it off into the darkness there in the corner, and just like that it was gone.

"I noticed you were lying there as stiff as a board and your eyes were wide open. I could see the whites reflected in the light. I came

Lost on Skinwalker Ranch

over to you and asked if you were okay. That's when I realized you were still dead to the world. I reached down to nudge your shoulder, not sure if it was safe to wake you, and that's when you sat up and started throwing hands."

I asked if I had hit him, and he said no. And that's when I caught a whiff of what smelled like wet dog. "You smell that?"

He said he wasn't smelling anything.

I sniffed a few times and so did Nick. "You don't smell that?"

And then he too caught it. "It smells kind of like stale toilet water, like when the bowl isn't venting properly, or maybe like..."

I cut him off, "Like wet dog."

"Yeah, like wet dog."

"Or like wet coyote."

"Could be wet coyote."

When we talked about it later that morning, Nick had told me that he couldn't sleep, so he went into the kitchen and was catching up on his emails. He's married and has four kids, the oldest in his first year of college. With no intentions of going back to bed, he had put on the coffee and was waiting for the coffeemaker to do its thing, looking up from the laptop every now and then impatiently. That's when he saw the shadow outside the door to my room.

According to him, it was as tall and as wide as most men. He described it as a shadow only in the sense that it was a dark apparition, but not projected two-dimensionally as would a normal shadow. This thing, he was certain, had mass to it, meaning form with depth and a shape.

When I asked him if there was any sense of presence, any feeling of dread or fear, anything like that; he said, "You would think that I would have felt its presence, something that real, something that big. But no, nothing. Had I not looked up, I wouldn't have known a thing."

Lost on Skinwalker Ranch

There was part of me that was thinking he was just fucking with the new guy, that it was a practical joke. But what would be the sense? There was only the two of us, so it wasn't like there was a third party to entertain. Isn't that the way it always is with practical jokers? There has to be an audience or it's all a waste of time. And besides, there was no getting around that there was a big, dark mass in the dream I was having and it was scary as shit.

Anyway, that's why the naps. It was either that, or give up sleeping and take to drinking to the point of passing out.

Lost on Skinwalker Ranch

10: Green and Purple In the Snow

We kept an eye out for coyote tracks over the next few days. The best we found was a lone trail down by the gulch. There's this one spot that the local wildlife uses to go across from one side to the next. Most of what's there are deer tracks and fox. I had yet to see an actual fox while I had been there, but I was told they're quite common. The coyote tracks were those of a single animal, and given their size compared to those that we followed to the homestead, probably from a female hunting mice or other rodents.

I guess the point I'm making is that we let our guard down—at least I did—and fell back to the usual routine. For those last few days we had been doing the rounds together, both during the day and at night. But that last night, the night where everything went to shit, we decided there was no danger in being apart, so we split the rounds with Nick going out to the two gates and I taking the mesa and the west end of the property.

Those were the arrangements I preferred. Doing the gates meant sitting in the SUV and waiting to see if any vehicles approached. It was boring and my ass was wide enough. At least doing the mesa meant climbing and walking. It's good exercise and tired me out so I'd sleep, which since that night with the shadow, I had to admit I was doing without much trouble. And like I said before, as long as you're moving, you really don't feel the cold.

We hadn't any fresh snow since Joan's husband found the coyote tracks. But it had been really cold, single digits at night, and the snow that was there had pretty much bricked over. The surface was hard and the snow below either powdery or grainy, depending on how deep. So there was no worry about your boots getting wet. The only

Lost on Skinwalker Ranch

real trick was not turning your ankle while stepping in the dark on any uneven spots that may have frozen over. I made sure my flashlight had a freshly charged battery and that the walkie-talkie was working fine—which it was.

I jumped in the SUV with Nick as he headed away from the trailer and towards the path to go to the east gate. He let me out over by the trail that goes up to the top of the mesa. We did a final radio check before he drove off. Everything was good.

The air that night was crisp and cold, but there was very little wind, if any at all, and the sky was dark and tall. The moon was big, but not full, and there were stars everywhere. I could make out the different constellations as clearly as if I was in a planetarium—just don't ask me to name them. That was one of the really neat things about being out here at night: there was so little in the way of ambient light, unlike Vegas where even on the clearest of nights only the brightest of stars are visible.

No sooner had I trekked up to the top of the trail, up to level ground, I caught the chirping of a coyote. If you've ever heard it, you know why I say chirping. Technically, it is more of a yip, but it's quick and sharp. I pointed the flash light in the direction of the sound, and although the brush up in that area is sparse, there's plenty of rock formation for the animals to stay out of sight. In fact, if I stood still and listened, there'd be the sounds of all kinds of critters scurrying about. Not seeing anything atop the rocks, I lowered the flashlight and let its white beam fan out across the ground out ahead of me. There was nothing.

My presence, however, hadn't scared off the coyote. As I walked towards the east end of the property, pretty much heading in the direction of Nick's position, the coyote continued its scavenging, nosing among the rocks for rodents, occasionally letting out one of those chirps, and each time sounding pretty much like it was in the same place and unconcerned with my being there.

Lost on Skinwalker Ranch

I keyed my radio and waited for Nick to acknowledge. With his mic open, I let him know I had a coyote up here. He asked if I wanted him to come up. But as it was only one, it wasn't necessary. I let him know It was otherwise quiet, not that I thought I'd come across any ghost hunters or paranormal investigators—whatever they call themselves—up here when it was this cold. Their vinyl tents aren't made for this kind of weather. I let Nick know that I'd spend a few more minutes up on the mesa and then start out towards the west gate. He told me to be careful and report back every fifteen minutes. It was standard procedure.

My stay on the mesa was brief. On the way down the trail I slipped on some poor footing and wound up sliding down on my ass for about ten feet or so. At first I was worried that I had sprained my ankle, or worse, broken it. But after the initial pain passed, I found I could put weight on it without any problem and that I could move it around pretty good. It pays to have quality boots and to lace them up tight.

The flashlight got bounced around too. As I went to the ground, I let it go, involuntarily, to brace my fall. I heard it skitter away to some spot below where my slide came to a halt. To make things more difficult, the light had gone out when it hit the ground and I had to use the glow of my cellphone to find it, which I did as it lay partially sticking up out of some rocks. I was relieved that it came back on with a shake. My first thought was that the light unit had broken. It would have meant going back to the trailer with only lighted windows to lead the way.

As I moved on to the dirt road, snow-packed tire tracks providing easy going, I keyed up Nick and let him know my position. He said he was going to hang at the east gate a while longer as twice already he had seen the glow of headlights, but both times the vehicle did a three-point turn out on the main road and before reaching the gate road, going back the way they came. He assumed they were simply drivers who realized they were going the wrong way. For those

Lost on Skinwalker Ranch

unfamiliar with the area, if you look on a map or a GPS, it looks like 7500 goes all the way through east to west. It doesn't show there's this huge ranch and private property in the way.

Down here below the ridge it was really quiet. I guess that should have told me something, because when things are normal there's always some kind of noise, even if it's just the sound of the nocturnal wildlife. Although you take it for granted, if you stop and listen, like I said before, at the very least you're going to hear hawks or owls. They both hunt at night and you can hear their wings or even their movement as they go from tree to ground or vice versa. Just because it's a desert doesn't mean it's not alive.

But not tonight. It was stone quiet as if everything was laying low and waiting for something to happen or because there was a large predator about, like a wolf. I had heard stories of wolves occasionally coming on to ranch properties after the livestock. And, of course, there were the cryptid stories of dog-men and canine-like creatures that were neither dog nor wolf—both or either of which, supposedly, were the source of those strange tracks Mark and I had tracked down to the gulch. That said, there was no livestock on this ranch and no reason for a wolf to be nosing about. So I kept walking and my ear tuned to my surroundings.

It takes a good half-hour to walk from the mesa trail to the homestead, so twice I had keyed in Nick and let him know my position. The first time I asked him if he noticed anything different, mentioning particularly what I had noticed about how quiet it was. He exited his vehicle and while seeking a strategic position kept talking to me. He told me he was moving toward the shallow creek bed at the base of the ridge so that he'd be more in the middle of things and likely to hear animal sounds. When he was satisfied he had the right spot, he said he'd get right back to me and keyed off. He takes things seriously like that. A couple of minutes later my walkie-talkie crackled and his voice came over to tell me all was status quo, meaning quiet,

Lost on Skinwalker Ranch

but a normal, every night kind of quiet. The critters were business as usual.

Not where I was. It was still too quiet. I assured him I'd keep him informed and keyed out.

The dirt road rounds to the left before it straightens on to the homestead. I was maybe ten or twelve strides around that bend when I saw the white of the snow up the road a way—right between the two homesteads—light up with a green and purple glow. When I say 'light up' I don't want you picturing this bright flash or if the snow was suddenly hit by a spotlight of some sort. It was hardly more than a reflection, like pale moonlight or watercolor with just enough paint to give it a hint of the green and a trace of purple barely visible at the edges. It was as if whatever was giving off the light wasn't very strong. To the left and right, the surface of the tree trunks and the bare branches reaching out over the road caught the reflection, giving them the appearance of leaping out from the darkness. I don't mind saying that it caught me off guard.

I immediately thought of Nick's description of the light he had seen. But I didn't see any dripping candle wax or four-foot long ripples in the night air opening up like a zipper in the dark. I had no doubt, though, that whatever it was that was glowing green and purple was off to one side or the other of the road and either coming from homestead one or two.

Not that it needs to be said, but by this time I had stopped walking. I keyed up the walkie-talkie, confident that this was definitely something that Nick would want to investigate; and to tell the truth, I wouldn't mind the company after experiencing the disappearing coyotes.

The walkie-talkie gave me nothing: no key-up, no crackle and no Nick. It had gone dead.

I had been told that there were power issues whenever there were paranormal entities in proximity: camera batteries losing power, watches stopping, cellphones not working, that kind of thing. I took

Lost on Skinwalker Ranch

off my glove so I could get to my cellphone. Sure enough, it too was dark. Shortly thereafter, the flashlight also flickered and went dark.

As a reflex, I reached to my hip and felt the solid mass of the pistol. I unsnapped the strap of the holster—and felt silly doing so. I could see myself explaining why I felt the need to shoot the Northern Lights.

There was still a couple hundred feet to go before the homestead and I started moving forward cautiously, all the while shifting my eyes from one side of the road to the other in search of the light source. While walking I repeatedly keyed the walkie-talkie, but without result. Then from the span of one moment to the next, I realized that it had gone dark. The greenish-purple glow was gone and the trees had receded back into the darkness. With nothing to focus on, I again stopped walking to let my eyes adjust. There was enough light from the stars and moon for me to walk safely, as long as I took my time to look where I was a stepping.

As I approached the tree line alongside the road out in front of homestead one—the old house north of the road—I saw this golden-yellow light. It was through the trees and towards the far end of the homestead. My first thought was that it was a flashlight, but I quickly changed my mind. First, the color was off—too golden—and the circumference was too big. Second, the light wasn't spreading away from the source like a flashlight beam would, but instead seemed to be contained within it. There was no bleed to the edges, if you know what I mean. If you've ever seen a lava lamp, well, it kind of looked like that, as if there was some sort of glowing substance inside a globe.

I was definitely intrigued and was sure I was experiencing my first real encounter with something alien or paranormal. Trying to make as little sound as possible, the snow surface crunching under my weight nonetheless, I moved into the tree line and staying as close to the tree trunks as I could, advanced to get a better line of sight. And that's when I saw the second one, almost identical in appearance to the first. It came from around the back of the house, moving like a balloon

Lost on Skinwalker Ranch

pulled by an invisible string. When it came within a few feet of the first one, it stopped and the two of them hung in place.

The only thing I could think to do was to pull out my phone and hope the thing was back to working. I kept my eye on the two orbs of light while removing my glove and reaching into my pocket for the device. I even searched for the power button without taking my eyes off them. And then in the fraction of a second it took me to glance down to see if the interface lit up and look back up, they were gone. Not only that, but the stupid phone didn't power-up either.

I stood still for a minute or two, hoping they'd reappear. But there was nothing. So I moved the rest of the way through the trees and on towards the homestead. I even went so far as to peer in through the old doorway and around through one of the windows towards the back. Without the flashlight, though, it was useless. Bigfoot could have been sitting inside taking a shit and I wouldn't have known any different.

My adrenalin rush fading, I gave up and decided I'd head back towards the east gate and the trailer, see if I could reach Nick by walkie-talkie. But no sooner did I come back around the house, I was hit simultaneously by an overwhelming sense of dread and the heavy stench of wet dog.

11: These are not Coyotes

The tree line was a good number of strides to my left and I had already made up my mind to take the path out onto the road where I would be out in the open. That's when I saw movement coming from the trees, two dark shapes, thin and upright. Had my flashlight been working, I would have shined it upon them, having no reason to believe it was anything but trespassers. But as they stepped into the clearing and into the moonlight, I near shit myself. This sick feeling hit me in the pit of my stomach and washed outward wobbling my legs, as if they were going to collapse beneath my weight. It was kind of like that feeling you get on the rollercoaster when it hits the first big drop and tickles you right down to the bladder. My vision went tunnel on me and it took all the training I could muster to not piss myself where I stood.

I want to say they looked like coyotes, sort of. Keep in mind, though, that at this point I wasn't trusting my own eyes or what my brain was telling me I was looking at. And it was dark, with only the pale illumination of moon and stars.

These things were almost my height, standing upright on skinny legs with bony, L-shaped knees—if they were knees at all—and up on their toes like spastic ballerinas. Their torsos were too long for their legs and emaciated as if they had never eaten. They had these round protruding bellies, almost like the kind you see on those starving kids in Africa, and the chest was angular as if looking down on a pointed roof, the skin—patchy with thin hair and scaled with mange—sucked in between the rib bones. Their arms weren't much different than the legs, elbows bony like the knees, only sticking out to the sides like chicken wings so that the forearms and paws—they definitely looked more paw than hand—were forced in towards the body and outward like kangaroo arms. There was no neck to speak of, as if their heads had been nestled haphazardly between the tapering shoulders, except

Lost on Skinwalker Ranch

they were jutting forward as if the things were craning to get a better look. Their muzzles were much shorter and weirder looking than you'd expect from canines, as if they were a sickly imitation of people, but still way too dog-like. Both had their lips drawn back in a half-snarl, half grin with yellow fangs showing. Their eyes reflected a jaundice yellow, the irises dark and beady. The ears were all canine, short and pointed. And there was no escaping that smell, like a raccoon that had been hit by a car, its three-day old carcass hidden by tall weeds but reeking in the summer heat. If you've had the experience, you know the smell.

Having some degree of sense and sanity yet remaining, I took the glove off on my right hand, my movements slow and controlled and taking care not to do anything that would startle and lead to attack. Reaching down to my side, I gripped and drew the pistol from the hip holster. As I did so, I started slowly stepping backwards thinking my best bet was the homestead. At the very least I would have the walls to my back.

As I took my first step back, the thing to my left responded by circling to its right—its movements spastic and ungainly, but quicker and with greater agility than I would have thought possible—and forcing me to turn to my left, leaving me exposed to the opposite side where the second one was.

No longer worried about them rushing me, I back pedaled as fast as I could to keep them both in my line of sight. It worked, as they both froze as if confused or maybe just being cautious. Still, they were both positioned so that I had to keep my head turning from side to side.

This is when I raised the gun up, hoping, I guess, that it would scare them. It usually works with people. No sooner did I do so, the thing on the left started advancing towards me, its head tilted to one side and bobbing up and down. The moon was to its back so that its eyes were little more than dark emptiness each side of its muzzle. Acting kind of out of instinct, the way you might do with a strange

Lost on Skinwalker Ranch

dog, I took a hard stomping step towards it and yelled. But it had no reaction of any sort and kept advancing, almost as if gliding across the snow. At about fifteen feet, I pointed the gun and fired—twice. The report of the shots was clear and crisp in the cold air; loud enough, I was hoping, for Nick to have heard. As for the bullets, I have no doubt that I hit it square in the upper torso with both shots. It stopped, but had no other reaction. Aware, obviously, that there was the other one to the other side, I turned and fired at the spot I had last seen it. It hadn't moved. That shot, too, had to be on target. It was no more than thirty feet away from me, even less. But it too showed no reaction.

At the moment, I was maybe be ten yards from the old house. Without thinking, I made a dash for the door. As I did so I glanced over my right shoulder to where the first thing was, the first one that I shot at. It hadn't moved and still had that stupid grin on its face. In stride and what seemed like slow motion, I reached the opening where the door had once been and leaped into the darkness. No sooner had my boot hit the surface of the floor, this large black mass rushed forward into my face. Before I could even get my hands up, I was hit by this stifling billow of air, only there was no air. It was as if I drew in a full breath of heavy soil or mud. My lungs expanded with a sudden heaviness. I couldn't exhale. I found myself gulping nothing. I started to panic—military experience or no—as the pressure built at my temples and the light headedness became dizziness and I had the sensation of spiraling downward. I was aware that my lungs were burning, but it was all so distant that it seemed more a curiosity than a worry, as was the undeniable fact that I was on the verge of losing consciousness.

But I didn't. At least I don't think I did. Sure there was a moment where everything went blank, as if someone turned off the record button in my brain. Then there was the fact that I was lying flat on my

Lost on Skinwalker Ranch

face, and it wasn't with my cheek against rotted wood. It was stone, rock, whatever you want to call it.

I let that realization register for a second before working on sitting up. When I felt ready, I took my time, expecting dizziness to get the better of me at any second. But I managed it without any ill feeling. Once to the seat of my pants, I pulled my knees in close, wrapped them with my forearms and rested my chin on my chest with my eyes closed. Believe it or not, I sensed without needing to look that I was there by myself and there was no immediate danger.

I don't know how long I sat there like that, a couple of minutes, maybe five. The first minute or so I was asking myself questions, the kind you would expect of someone establishing his sanity. I was confident I knew my name, my birthdate, my address, who my parents were, the names of my siblings, where I had been before I wound up here. And that was all good. Right up to the 'where am I and how did I get here' part. Those were two questions I had no answers for. The only thing that made sense was that I had lost consciousness for longer than I thought and someone or something brought me here—wherever here was. It was that thought that made me open my eyes and lift my head.

As I had expected—don't ask me why—I was in a cave of sorts, almost like a chamber or a hall. It was long and narrow and I was towards the shorter end, more or less in the middle of the floor. At first, I was limited to squinting and found myself blinking a lot and squeezing my eyes tight for seconds at a time. I thought maybe there was something wrong with my eyes, either that or my brain was seeing things kind of funny. Everything was awash in amber. If you've ever noticed how objects at night appear in varying shades of grey, or if you've watched old black and white movies, that's what this was like; only it was amber and not grey.

And it wasn't just the light—I say light because it would have been pitch black in there otherwise, but my depth perception was off too. I couldn't tell how far away the walls were or how high the stone above

Lost on Skinwalker Ranch

my head. No matter where I looked, ceiling, floor, walls, it was all too close and too far away at the same time. It was disorienting and made my queasy.

I managed to stand up without puking and turned around to have a look in the opposite direction. From what I could tell, and if my eyes weren't playing tricks on me, the chamber floor sloped subtly downward, while at the same time the walls grew narrower and the ceiling lower. It had a claustrophobic feel to it and gave me the sickening thought that I had been entombed with no way out. But then there down at the end and along the right hand wall, floor to ceiling, was a dark line that stood out in contrast to the rest. It gave me hope.

Before I headed down that way, I did a quick personal survey to make sure I was all there and in one piece. I didn't detect any blood, dried or otherwise, and there was nothing particular giving me pain or discomfort of any sort. So I had to assume no broken bones. My ankle felt a little stiff, but then I remembered I had lost my footing coming off the mesa. I took that as a sign that I hadn't completely lost my mind. But then I realized I only had one glove, and worse, no gun. The glove I could do without—in fact, being without it made me take note that I wasn't cold, or even hot for that matter—but the gun, that left me feeling naked.

I looked around to see if there was anything I could arm myself with. That too was odd. There was nothing there in the chamber, not even a rock or stone on the ground. The whole place, at least from where I stood and from what I could see in this fucked-up light, looked to have been swept clean. All I had were my bare hands and the hope that those two coyote things were someplace else, not to mention whatever it was that had been waiting for me there in the homestead.

I set off towards the other end and could definitely feel the downward slope of the floor in my calves and knees. I must have taken maybe twelve, fifteen strides when it struck me that I wasn't

Lost on Skinwalker Ranch

making any progress in terms of getting any closer to where I wanted to go. It was as if I was on a treadmill, walking but going nowhere. So I did what anyone else would do, I started walking faster. But all that did was make things worse. I was just going nowhere faster. So I stopped, took a deep breath and turned to look behind me. Fucked-up depth perception or not, I was certain I wasn't in the same place where I started. To convince myself I was actually moving, I turned to the right and walked straight at the chamber wall. Two strides, three strides, four strides and nothing; I was going nowhere. Just as I was about to despair—something I don't do—I stepped forward determinedly and like that, the wall rushed up to me and I almost smashed my nose and teeth right into solid stone.

But the truth is, of course, the wall never moved. It was always there, solid and stationary. Had I been running, I would have knocked myself out. The best I could figure, it was some kind of visual illusion, the light playing with my brain, the way the brain sees things.

To help me keep my shit together, I started walking again, but this time with my hand running along the stone of the wall. The sensation of my fingertips tracing along the rock kept me oriented and convinced that I was covering ground. It didn't occur to me until later how smooth the wall was, not like sheetrock, but strangely so for it to be Mother Nature's doing only.

I don't know how long I was walking. There was absolutely no sense of time in that chamber and my watch, which showed a few minutes before ten, no doubt stopped working about the same time as my cellphone, my flashlight and my walkie-talkie, all three of which were still in my possession, the little good it was doing me.

What I was aware of, however, was how much the space had closed in around me. I could feel it without even looking. The rock ceiling was no more than a half-foot above my head and it took me only a short slide step to run my fingers along the opposite wall. And that's how I found the end: my right hand without warning stabbed into nothing.

Lost on Skinwalker Ranch

Not expecting it, I was startled and pulled back abruptly causing my left shoulder to plow into the angled intersection of the far wall and the rock face at the end. Once I reoriented myself and figured out what happened, I could see that the rock in front of me wasn't straight across, but was actually angled to the right and leading into another tunnel.

The tunnel itself opened with a flat surface very much like a landing, but it was not lighted, which would explain why it looked dark from the other end of the chamber. Beyond the landing, though, it was illuminated and with that same amber aura. Only what came next wasn't a flat slope. Instead there were stairs—narrow and shallow—that had been chiseled into the stone and down was the only way they went.

12: Half-Light

I do consider myself a man's man, but there are two things that I avoid if I can help it. One is heights. I don't mind being in high places, like on top of buildings or up on the mesa, for example. Up on an extended ladder or up in a tree—that's a different story. Two is closed- in places. And this was a closed-in place. Not only were the walls tight—so much so that if I was careless I would brush my shoulders—but the ceiling felt like it was pressing down on me. There were long stretches where I had to keep my hand held out in front of my forehead and constantly duck so as not to scrape my head on the stone above.

My initial perception was that this tunnel, if you want to call it that, started out as no more than a fissure that Mother Nature had opened in the granite, and then some primitive people—little people—came along and did the engineering.

The steps were very awkward to navigate. Although they were consistent one to the next, they weren't very deep, only three or four inches each, and not as long as my boots, so that more often than not I was landing on my heels or short-stepping to put my foot down like a normal step. It was distracting and laborious.

Making things worse, I was having that same perception issue. I was clearly walking downward, and though the tunnel drifted left and right now and then, more often than not, I had a line of sight suggesting I was getting a good look at the way ahead. Nonetheless, I couldn't tell with any certainty how much ground I was covering. It got to the point where I was counting steps. But other than giving me a sense of being in control, it wasn't doing me any good. The only proof I had that I was actually going anywhere was when I would come to one of those places where the tunnel shifted. The shifts,

Lost on Skinwalker Ranch

however, were never sharp or sudden, but more like the ragged edges of an uneven tear.

Forget about any concept of time. I had no idea how long I had been on those stairs, and even started thinking that I was somehow going in circles, that maybe there was an opening I missed. I even wondered aloud if unknowingly I had entered some type of maze.

I think for the first time in my life I was on the verge of panic. It was a sick feeling of helplessness I never want to experience again. Using everything I had ever been taught about dealing with being in desperate situations, I sat down on a step and took a mental survey. I acknowledged I was alone—for all I knew inside some cave within the ridge, without food or water, no weapons and with no idea where I was heading. On the positive side, I had a direction in which to go—I think, there was air and it wasn't cold. In fact, it wasn't hot, either. I'm not even sure there was a temperature. In fact, that I could detect, there wasn't any air movement at all. Yet my breathing was fine.

It was while I was sitting there getting my mental shit together that I noticed the wall art. What freaked me out was that, now that I was seeing them, they had been chiseled and etched into both sides of the walls the whole length of the tunnel. Not believing it at first, that I could have missed them this entire time, I went back up the stairs a distance, and sure enough, they were there, and probably all the way back to the beginning.

The etchings—not quite floor to ceiling—appeared to be some sort of prehistoric story board, the same figures repeated over and over again in the same sequence and in two different scenes; all basic geometrical shapes with little detail.

The first scene started with what I assumed was a regular person. The legs were little more than elongated rectangles and the torso v-shaped, wider at the shoulders than the hips. The head was a simple oval, scratched into the stone without eyes or mouth. There was no neck to speak of. Then came a canine. There was no mistaken it: rear legs, ears, muzzle and teeth and down on all-fours. Maybe it was a

Lost on Skinwalker Ranch

wolf, maybe a coyote or a dog. The third was the weird one. It appeared to be neither man nor canine, but some combination of the two. It had the same v-shaped torso, but the ears were definitely canine, the head level at the top and barely protruding above the shoulders. There were no facial features.

The second scene was centered round this ominous figure with attributes that were clearly not human. Fully upright, its body had wide, rounded shoulders which tapered in unbroken lines down to the feet. There were no distinguishable arms or legs. The head was skull-shaped with large round and pupil-less eyes. There was some sort of weird tubular shit that looked almost like ram horns coming out of the top of the head. It looked to me to be standing before some sort of opening. Drawn at its feet were multiple prone figures crudely shaped like gingerbread men—only etched like skeletons. No doubt they were supposed to be dead. Then there were others, similarly drawn, but upright—dead but standing, like zombies or the walking dead. Towards the outer edges of the scene were other figures much like the one in the middle, only with less detail and not as fantastic. Here and there was some other stuff that may have been the flames of a fire, like a campfire, and what looked to be urns or jars, the clay kind.

The fact that these drawings were even here gave me confidence that there had to be a way out, as long as the tunnel hadn't collapsed up ahead. Getting back on my way, the stairs yet descending, I saw these same two scenes repeating themselves without end, one after the other, both sides of the walls, and with little variance—only enough to guess they had been put there by hand and probably by the same person or persons.

I had given up trying to keep track of time, or even counting how many steps I had taken. If I had to take a guess, I'd say—and this without exaggeration—more than five-thousand. And I'll tell you why: I have a treadmill at home that I use routinely, mostly walking. Running on those things kills my knees. Anyway, the point is I usually

Lost on Skinwalker Ranch

do 30 minutes on level three. That's a mile and one half, which comes out to about 3500 steps. I know; I've counted them. What else is there to do on a treadmill? Now I know these steps were considerably shorter than the strides I take on the machine, but even so it would still translate to more than a mile, considering how far I had already come.

Just as I was starting to get that panic feeling again, that feeling of despair that puts a knot in your stomach and crowds your brain, I missed a step and stumbled. The stair had come to an abrupt end and the ground went suddenly level. I had been putting my foot down at four inch intervals for so long, that it had become mindless. But this time, instead, I caught the tip of my boot and pitched forward. The only reason why I didn't fall flat on my face was because I was able to get my hands and arms extended before me. I immediately felt the grit of sand and soil grind into my palms.

I went down upon one knee, my right one, and looked up. I was no longer in the tunnel, but out in a canyon enclosed all around—at least from where I could see—with stone walls scaling up I don't know how far. Although I was beneath an open sky, that amber light hadn't changed any and I still couldn't figure out how far I might be away from something that I wasn't already on top of.

For example, there was scrub brush and low rock formation all around me. Just to make sure it was real, I went over to the nearest bush and grabbed at the leaves. They held tight to the branch, and though they felt funny to the touch—like leaves in autumn just before they start to turn color, they were real and alive. I pulled at one expecting it to come free. But it held stubbornly and I had to tug at it a couple more times before I finally plucked it. What was fucked up is that it made no sound when it snapped from the spidery twig to which it was clinging. Looking it over, it was nothing special, other than no matter how I turned it, it gave no indication of the green color I was sure was there. Everything was shades of amber.

Lost on Skinwalker Ranch

Before going any further, I tried to get my bearings, first by looking up into the sky over my head and then all around me as to decide on a direction to go.

I had mentioned earlier that the sky around the ranch reminded me of a planetarium, but because of the clarity of the stars and not the idea of a dome over your head. But that was not the case here. First, there were no stars. Not any that I could see. It was all cloud cover, just without the clouds. It was more like a thin blanket of fog or mist with the sense, if not the actual appearance, of spiraling ever so slowly, if just perceptively, counter-clockwise. It was as if the whole of the heavens were contained within an upside-down bowl placed on top of the rim of the canyon. It was at the same time both mesmerizing and making me seasick. It was all I could do to look away.

I decided to concentrate on the canyon walls, instead. Like I said, they were all around me, but I couldn't say if one side was closer than the other, or if walking straight ahead was the better of the plans. The voice inside me wanted me to take the shortest route, which meant to one side or the other, if only to reach out and touch the stone, make sure it was really there. But I wanted to believe that my time in the tunnel taught me something. So I decided straight to the other end was the way to go, keeping me eyes open for anything that would suggest a way out.

I meandered through the scrub and rock, going wherever the path was leading. That meant sometimes to the left, sometimes to the right, others round-about or snaking this way and that. There were even trails which ran straight on for a while. I say trails because someone or something had been passing through here probably for centuries.

My aim was fairly obvious: I was making for the other end of the canyon and looking for a way out or a way up. Nagged by that same feeling that I wasn't making any progress, I got in the habit of stopping every now and again to turn and look back from where I had

Lost on Skinwalker Ranch

come to make sure I was leaving some sort of mark in the grainy soil. And I was.

I was distracted thinking about the fact that by now I should be feeling something in the way of hunger, or at the very least, thirst. I hadn't eaten since dinner, which was around 7:00, and the last thing I had to drink was a bottle of water before heading out on patrol. But I was feeling neither of those things, and I found it odd. And that's when I noticed that the trail I was navigating had brought me as close as I had yet been to the canyon walls. There on my left, and for the first time, I saw what were clearly cave dwellings—first one and then another, and then another again, one above the other like some sort of prehistoric condo complex.

Not that I had actually seen any before, not in real life. But I had seen artwork and documentaries, things like that. This was no different. These weren't just holes or openings in the rock, they were somebody's home, dwellings where people had at one time lived. The only thing missing was the tree limb ladders, the reed-woven baskets and hanging blankets.

I glanced ahead to see where the trail ran and saw that if I stayed with it I should get closer. From where I was, the face of the rock looked almost as if it had been painted on some huge, flat surface. Among everything else I could see, this was the darkest in color—a pale, flat gold. But there was no contrast to show what must surely be an infinite number of indents, surface ridges and bumps, the kind of irregularities you'd expect of rock and stone. It was a very alien, very unnatural.

I continued where the trail took me and as I covered ground I could make out, first in the lower dwellings and then in those above, a sort of dim illumination within. The more steps I took, the more I swore I saw a flickering, like the kind you'd associate with flame dancing along firewood. What more could I think but that it was a trick of the lighting, whatever source it was that caused everything to go amber?

Lost on Skinwalker Ranch

Anyway, the way I saw it, if there was fire, there had to be people. I threw all semblance of self-control out the window and started to jog towards what I perceived as the closest cave with a flickering inside. Faster and faster, I picked up the pace unconcerned that I was running in place. At any time I fully expected to stumble in upon whoever was at home.

But even here where air was unnecessary, as it were, my lungs started to burn and I could feel a stitch gripping at my side. Trying to ignore the building discomfort, I kept my legs moving as fast as they would go.

Stubborn as I wanted to pretend I was, however, I had to stop. If I didn't I was going to pass out, or at the very least, collapse to the ground. And that's when I saw the silhouette, or maybe it was a shadow, drift across the cave opening and fold against the far wall. There was someone in there, and by the looks of it, it was upright and human.

Lost on Skinwalker Ranch

13: Little People

I calmed myself and started walking again, this time keeping the pace to a steady stride. Wherever the fuck I was—and this wasn't the time to try and figure it out, running or walking, it made no difference. If I was going to get somewhere it was because that's where I was going. In other words—I had no control over it.

The whole place was a like a trick of mirrors, an infinite number of them all precisely arranged and angled so that the multitude of reflections layered so perfectly one upon the other that they together cast a single image. No matter where or how I moved, I felt like I was, at the same time, both further away and closer to the place from where I started and the place to where I was going. It was maddeningly disorienting and making me queasy.

To keep my thinking straight, I kept my eye on that one dwelling in which I saw the silhouette and the shadow it cast. And though the glow within continued to flicker as if with flame, and even then barely perceptively, there was nothing else to see.

Just as I started to admonish myself for letting my imagination and desperation get the better of me, I saw movement out of the side of my eye to the right. Turning, I know I saw the figure of a man along the base of the rock face take an easy stride and pass into a dwelling at ground level not too far from where I was.

I called out, just a "hey!" But it was as if my voice fell out of my mouth and went mute to the dirt at my feet. To my own ears it sounded as if it came from far away and with only enough strength to reach me, little more than recognizable as someone yelling. So strange it was, I actually turned back to the distance, thinking that there really was someone else out there and they were trying to get my attention.

But I know what I saw. Committed, I stayed to the trail as it took me parallel to the canyon face and the dwellings, both high and low in the rocks. Every one of them held the same glow with the same sense

Lost on Skinwalker Ranch

of dancing flames. And as if there was something or someone playing a cruel joke on me, there was always enough of a glimpse of some silhouette or shadow so that I'd have no choice but to think someone was home.

More than once I saw what appeared to be the form of a man—definitely Indian (don't ask me how I knew)—either standing stationary in the middle of the dwelling entrance, if only for a moment, or entering from outside. There was even one, a lower dwelling, ground level, in which I know I saw the shadows of what looked to be three Indian women seated upon the floor and working at some domestic task, perhaps weaving baskets or stringing fish to dry; I don't know. There was no way to be sure as the whole of it was little more than forms of dark amber, flat and elongated, moving upon the inner wall of stone.

Again and again, I shouted and with the same result. My voice, thin and distant, failing to carry over to the dwellings or receive any acknowledgement. Here I was in the middle of some fantastic Indian village carved out of the stone of the canyon, surrounded by silhouettes and shadows going about their daily routine, oblivious to my presence and beyond my reach.

Resigned and succumbing to despair, I sat in the dirt with my back to a low rock formation facing the canyon wall. There was scrub brush fairly thick to both sides and a bunch to the back. It gave me the sense of shelter, though against what, I don't know. There was no wind or weather and I had not seen or heard anything that would suggest wildlife. It probably served some primal need more than anything else. Not wanting to go any further, at least not at that moment, I closed my eyes, thinking perhaps that I'd get a little sleep and then think things out later.

Maybe I nodded out for a minute or two. I can't be sure. Nevertheless, a dissonant hum, the first sound other than my own voice I had heard while lost, caught my attention. I can't say if it originated out of the depths of an REM stage and that's what woke

Lost on Skinwalker Ranch

me, and then it just happened to be real. Or if it was the sound, real and not just in my head, that woke me—had I actually been sleeping. Regardless, other than to say that it was like a cacophony of low voices distant and murmuring, there was nothing I understood as actual words. Tilting my head in an attempt to get a better read, it seemed to me to be coming from directly overhead, there at the top of the upside-down bowl.

I sat there, my arms wrapped around my knees and my head resting back against the stone, listening to the voices drone on. It was unchanging, steady and rhythmic like a chant, with shape and form that carried both vowel and consonant sounds. I tried to listen for a pattern, something that would suggest, if not familiar words, at least the type of syllabication you'd expect from someone repeating the same thing over and over again, like the chorus of a simple song or, well, chanting.

I stared straight overhead as if by concentrating all of my attention to where I thought it was coming from, I'd hear it better. I can't say if it actually made any difference, but I do know that I suddenly realized I was timing the beat, the rhythm, with but the merest hint of my body rocking back and forth. And though I couldn't reproduce the chant with any accuracy, I was mimicking the syllabication and phonetics in my head. If it was a chorus, it was four syllables repeated four times and then five different syllables repeated twice, and then start again, all with vowel sounds, but not all with consonants. The fact that it had to be coming from an intelligent source, a human source, gave me a renewed spirit and the motivation to get back on my feet and find a way out of this place.

I hadn't noticed when I sat down—all of my attention up to that point focused on the canyon wall and the dwellings—that I had made significant headway towards the other end of the canyon from which I entered. For the first time I saw that it was not fully enclosed, at least not with the same tall ridge. There at the other end was what appeared to be a relatively low mesa, discernible more by a narrowing rectangle

Lost on Skinwalker Ranch

of a slightly lighter shade of amber which gave the impression of a plane than anything physical. And that became my goal.

As I walked, I tried not to think of my destination in terms of distance but eventuality. Nevertheless, I went back to counting strides, one after the next falling in rhythm with the voices which followed overhead.

The more I walked and the more time passed, which it did whether perceived or not, I wondered as to the absence of anything resembling hunger or thirst. At first, I attributed it to adrenalin and the distraction of being lost and trying not to panic. But at this point, particularly, I felt oddly calm and at ease; and not only that, but if I was going to feel either it would be when I was thinking about it. As much as I traced my lips with my tongue or sought to gather and swallow my own saliva, I managed nothing in the way of measurable moisture. Yet I felt nothing in the way of thirst. Hunger was the same. I had no feeling of emptiness nor pangs of any sort.

That's when it hit me—I mean really hit me—that not only was I not hearing anything that would indicate wildlife or even insects—not the chirp of a cricket, the peep of a bird, no flapping of wings nor unseen rodents scuttling through the brush—but that beyond the sound of my own boots on the soil—muted in the same way as my attempts to yell—I was hearing nothing at all. Nothing. It was as if I had been placed under glass or inside a sea shell. Only the murmuring chant, which I could not escape, kept me from thinking that I had gone deaf.

Lost in my thoughts, trying to reconcile things I could not explain, I was a number of strides along before I noticed I was on some sort of road. I say road because it was clear that significant engineering had been done to clear away all brush and stone and to level the bedrock to produce clean lines to both sides, and these, the best I could make it, some thirty feet or so apart. Unlike the stairs which brought me here into the canyon, I could feel in my steps a slight incline as if I was on a ramp of sorts.

Lost on Skinwalker Ranch

Again, this little change in my predicament lifted my spirits and renewed my energy. I picked up the pace of my walking and blocked all negative thought from my mind. The chanting by now had become little more than ambient noise and I had to remind myself that it was still there.

But that too changed.

My counting of steps had just passed 800, each one ever so slightly uphill, when the drone of distant and foreign voices was replaced one stride to the next by a single one, louder and definitely nearby. I had heard Navajo often enough that I was sure this was something close, only more ancient and with an intonation that carried ominous notes. There behind it was the sharp clack of wood on wood, as if someone was beating alternately on a section of tree trunk with ritualistic fervor.

There was no reason to leave the road as there was only one way to go. So I followed it, the intensity of the chant and the drumming remaining the same. Without warning, the ground, still level and smooth, pitched abruptly upward and the ramp came to an end. As if rearing up before me out of nowhere there was a set of stairs, wide side to side, but each step narrow and shallow, cut deep into the rock and leading upwards towards the ridge top.

I hesitated, none too thrilled with my last staircase experience. But what choice did I have? Unless I was going back the way I came, there was nowhere else to go. So I started up.

The stairs themselves were so shallow that I started taking them two at a time, staying off my heels and taking care to set my steps so that I could feel through my boots all my weight on the ball of my feet. I had taken so many steps that I started counting again just so that I'd have a sense of how far I was going.

Finally, I reached an open area in the rock, to the left of which and slightly taller than the top of my head there was an opening. It had the look of a long fissure stretching across the face of the rock, fifty or sixty feet long and maybe seven feet high towards the center,

Lost on Skinwalker Ranch

somewhat less to each side. All the way to the left was what appeared to be stone altar and I could make out the shape of the body upon it.

Here where I stood, the chanting was considerably louder, as was the drumming. Figuring my only way out of here was to make my presence known, yet wanting to be cautious, I moved closer. As I did so, I looked around to see if there was a way up.

All the way to the right, there was a ramp cut into the very rock of the cliff face. Keeping below the height of the ledge of the opening, I made my way over to it. Listening at first to see if I had been detected, and hearing no letup in either the chanting or the drumming, I started up the ramp. The surface was smooth and even.

Not sure if I should show myself or stick with the more cautious approach, I opted for the latter, crouching low and staying as close to the rock face as possible. My plan was to take up a position just to the right of the fissure opening and get a look inside.

I made it to the spot I had chosen without being seen. Squatting down, I pressed my back to the stone and poked my head around only enough so I could see in. The structure I thought was an altar was exactly that. There was what appeared to be a body laid out on top of it, but whether man or woman, girl or boy, I couldn't tell. It had been wrapped head to toe in some sort of a swathing, and from the looks of it, the feet were in my direction.

I also noticed, if not as immediately as I should have, that everything was in shades of grey and shadow, not the amber, and the only illumination was emanating from a low burning fire somewhere deeper in the opening than I could see from my current position.

There between the fire and the altar were two figures, near naked from what I could tell. But as the light was behind them, they were little more than silhouettes. One was kneeling before the cylindrical instrument he was beating upon, which from the looks of it was no more than a section of tree trunk somewhat hollowed out for the purpose. I say somewhat because the sound was a solid clunk and not the booming sound you'd expect. The way he was seated, one side of

Lost on Skinwalker Ranch

his face was reflecting the pale glow of the fire. He looked as if his face had been smeared with dry earth, the contrast of light and dark making his nose look wide and flat. I couldn't make out any other details.

The second figure was the one chanting. He was dancing in place with his feet hoping from the ground alternately and slow as if he was really tired or really old, or both. I couldn't help but notice how short he was—maybe 'four feet—and that his arms hung almost to the ground, like some sort of half-man, half-orangutan. Clearly, it was some sort of ritual and probably for the dead guy.

I'm not sure how long I crouched there watching, not wanting to interrupt what was going on. It's also more than possible that I too was drawn into a trance-like state. It's not a far-fetched notion given the rhythmic chanting and the unchanging beat.

Regardless, though, out of nowhere this dark form suddenly took shape there within the fire ring as if standing right in the middle of what remained of the burning embers. Tall and foreboding, I couldn't help but think of the thing in my dreams.

For a moment, I thought I was the only one who noticed. The one that was drumming never missed a beat nor looked up from what he was doing. Deep in his self-induced trance, he was oblivious to the danger. But the little man dancing stopped his jumping-about midstep. His chanting, however, intensified, taking on a more urgent tempo and tone.

Not able to take my eyes from the fire ring, I watched as the darkness deepened and gathered a more definite form. As it did, I was near overtaken by a sudden sense of dread that shivered my bladder and filled me with a fear the likes of which I had never experienced before. I gagged against an overwhelming stench of something dead and a dank thickness which swelled my tongue.

Just as my head went light and I started to swoon, I saw the little dancing man unfold his long arms with a flourish out towards the fire as if tossing flowers into the sea. There was a blinding flash that flared

Lost on Skinwalker Ranch

over the fire pit cascading sparks and smoke in every direction. And just before everything went black on me, I saw the body on the altar sit straight up, the shrouded cloth concealing its face drawn into a wide open mouth as it gasped for a breath.

Lost on Skinwalker Ranch

14: Found

I came back to the real world with some guy's hands tight on my shoulders and pressing me down into a bed. He was telling me everything was good, doing his best to sound reassuring while he held me in place. As much as I might have wanted to—and it was more reflex than anything else—I didn't have the strength to resist. My head was foggy, I had that same queasy feeling, my arms felt dead, I was breathing heavily and I was completely disoriented. I had no idea where I was.

As it turned out, I was in a hospital room and the guy with his hands on me was a medical intern of some sort. Apparently, while he was bedside and checking the I-V needle stuck in my forearm, I bolted up out of unconsciousness or deep sleep, perhaps a combination of the two, and started throwing punches at an invisible foe. Needless to say, the needle came out and the machine monitoring my vital signs shot up to ridiculous numbers, the adrenaline rush sending my pulse rate up to the one-forties. Not wanting me to do myself harm or anyone else, he grabbed my arms, pushed me back and restrained me.

The intern, I think he said his name was Aubrey, was all for giving me some type of sedative to calm me down, insisting the rest would do me good. But I talked him out of it. By the time the nurse showed up with the two little plastic cups, one with water and one with the magical pill, the monitor had convinced the Aubrey guy that I was okay, and so he waved her off, but not before taking the two cups. He placed them side by side on the little table at the head of my bed, telling me they would be there if I were to have a change of mind.

Anyway, he didn't have all that much information for me, confirming only that I was in a local hospital—I won't say which one—and that I had been brought in by ambulance only a short while ago. He indicated the I-V bag with a nod of his head, the needle of

Lost on Skinwalker Ranch

which he had since reinserted and taped into place. It was still 4/5ths of the way full. Other than that, he couldn't say what the deal was.

When I asked him if there was anything to worry about, meaning was there anything wrong with me, he reached for the clipboard he had at hand, shrugged indifferently, and said, "A little dehydrated, but other than that, I don't see anything all that serious."

I did, however, manage to get out of him that a couple of guys had been there to check me in and that they were told to come back in a few hours. He then suggested I try to get some sleep, let the I-V do its job, and added that someone would come along to check on me later.

After he left, I had a change of mind and decided the sedative might not be a bad idea after all.

I wound up sleeping for almost ten hours. When I came out of it I had the pressing urge to take a piss and I was incredibly hungry—two sensations which had been missing of late. Fortunately, the I-V had been removed and I was free to make my way to the bathroom. It wasn't until I came back to the bed that I noticed the clock said it was past 7:30. I could tell it was PM and not AM because there was darkness the other side of the windows, the blinds only partially drawn.

Apparently, I had slept through meal time. The nurse that responded to the buzzer promised she would do what she could to find me something to eat. As she made to leave, she turned as if she had suddenly remembered something, and said, "You had visitors earlier. But as you were dead to the world, they said they'd be back tonight." She glanced at her watch and added, "Visiting hours are almost over. I bet they're on their way up as we speak."

I nodded and smiled. Dead to the world—if she only knew.

Nick and this other guy, Paul, one of the home office power players, showed up a little after 8:00. It was good to see a familiar face—not that I had ever met Paul, and since the nurse seemed to have

Lost on Skinwalker Ranch

forgotten about me, even better that Nick had a bag from McDonald's.

"I thought you'd appreciate this," he said, coming through the door and flipping me the bag.

I could smell the fries.

He introduced Paul, who extended his hand. We shook and he told me he did some investigating for BAASS when needed. I didn't say anything, but caught the change in his tone when he said 'needed'.

While I made short work of two cheeseburgers and the large fries, Nick and Paul filled me in on what I wanted to know.

As I listened, it sounded like they were talking about some other guy. According to the way they were telling it—mostly Nick, I had been AWOL for about 80 hours, give or take. Nick said he heard the gun shots some time short of 23:00—that's 11:00 PM for you civilians. Unable to raise me on the walkie-talkie, he raced toward the homestead in the SUV. Not knowing how far I had come from off the mesa, he abandoned it just beyond the tractor and took to foot. Using his flashlight, he tracked my boot prints to the tree line out front of homestead one. It didn't take any investigative expertise to see that I had cut through the trees. As he passed into the clearing, he saw that my prints were mixed there in the snow with others that were elongated and clearly not mine. He admitted that it took him a few minutes before he realized that I had backed off in the direction of the homestead.

"I could see by the prints and the lengths of your stride that you had turned and started to run," he said, stating the obvious. "I had no reason to think that you wouldn't still be inside and was more worried that you'd take a shot at me. Imagine my surprise when my calls went unanswered and I went in to find only empty space and a glove."

After that, he came back out and with only the limited reach of the flashlight, he managed to follow the tracks of the coyote things—I had described them to him and Paul—back across the road to homestead two, where again they just disappeared. There were,

Lost on Skinwalker Ranch

however, no signs of me. My tracks went no further than the clearing between the tree line and the homestead. And while there were clear indications of my presence there inside the house, there was nothing indicating I had left.

That, of course, was no surprise to me. I knew I hadn't left, not in the way they were thinking, not out through the front door. While Nick was searching around in the snow for boot prints, I was in a stone chamber beneath the ridge—a detail I decided to keep to myself, at least for the moment.

Not wanting to leave me out there, certain that I was somewhere in the vicinity and perhaps hurt, Nick put in a call to the house and had Joan get the local police out to the ranch. But with very little to go on, all they could do was search the property—which they did. Needless to say, they didn't turn up anything.

Following the search, which took well into the early morning, the local officers departed and promised to return once the sun came up. Nick went back to the trailer and put in an immediate call to the home office. Of course, they had a different perspective on what may have happened, meaning something paranormal, and told Nick they'd have somebody out here without delay. That somebody was Paul. Two other members of the security team also came to help with the search, neither of whom I had met. One was Ryan and the other Greg.

As the last place I was known to be was homestead one, come daylight that's where they started the search, and when my gun was found. Apparently, after I dropped it, it had fallen between the rotted floor boards. Nick had missed it the first time around, but not with the light of day filtering in.

Turning up nothing else, as was so with the rest of the search, they decided to set a watch, one person or another sitting in the SUV in the middle of the road between the two homesteads, basically around the clock. The only time the area was not monitored was when the shift would change and whoever was out there would drive the SUV back to the trailer to let the next guy take over and drive back.

Lost on Skinwalker Ranch

That's how they found me, just before nine this morning, and more than three days after I had disappeared.

The routine was that the guy taking the change in shift would drive out along the dirt road, park the SUV between the two homesteads, exit the vehicle and make a physical inspection of both homes. My understanding it was one of the other guys, Greg, I think, who found me.

"I know it wasn't me," laughed Nick. "I was back here in the trailer with Paul when the call came in. You were found in homestead one. The guy stuck his head in through the door and you were there flat on the floor, one leg stretched out before you and the other with the foot through the floor boards. You were clearly out of it, but definitely breathing and otherwise looking normal. We called the wagon and, well, here you are."

I listened but not much of it was making any sense, not if you were seeing things from where I stood. According to what they were saying, there were absolutely no signs of any fresh prints in the snow outside the homestead that would suggest I had walked in from the outside.

"Absolutely not possible," said Paul, no room for doubt in his tone. "We had been in and out of that place four or five times each, more than twenty times all told. However you got in there, it wasn't from the outside, not when we found you. And there is no way you were in there at any time during the time you were unaccounted for."

To add to the strangeness, Paul said, according to the doctor, when I was brought in, my core temperature was normal. His guess, meaning the doctor, was that I couldn't have been out there for more than a handful of minutes. Yet, according to everything else, I was gone—missing—for more than 80 hours.

"It's not possible," Paul repeated, "that anyone would be out in that cold for more than three days and yet be as warm as those two burgers you just ate." He looked over at Nick, "What was it, five

Lost on Skinwalker Ranch

below, ten below last night. And it hasn't been out of the twenties the whole time that I've been here."

Nick nodded, "Mid-twenties at the best."

That next morning, Nick was waiting for me in the lobby to take me back to the ranch, at least for now. Arrangement had already been made for me to fly home to Las Vegas. But before I went, there were two "scientists" from BAASS that were on their way out and the guy with the brogue wanted me to walk them through what had happened that night.

Now, keep in mind, up to this time, I hadn't told anyone any of what I had gone through; and oddly enough, other than general questions, no one had asked. That didn't change in the SUV. Nick only asked how I was feeling and made a comment about "strange shit that happens on the ranch".

However, once we were back in the trailer, Paul asked me if I was up to going on record. He showed me his cellphone which he was going to use to record what I had to say.

Had I been somewhere else or with anyone other than these guys, I probably would have played dumb, made out like I had amnesia or some shit. But the fact was this is why we're here. UFO and paranormal stuff.

So we made a pot of coffee and I let it flow. I left out nothing.

It was just Paul, Nick and me. The other two guys, Greg and Ryan, were out doing the rounds. I told them about the chamber, the stairs, the drawings, the open canyon, the dwellings, the silhouettes and shadows, the unintelligible voices, the road, the shit in the cavern with the two little people and the dark figure, the amber thing and the thing with perception and sound, the feel of the air, the temperature and not feeling either hunger or thirst. All of it. For the most part, they both sat there listening and sipping from their coffee cups, interrupting only a handful of times to ask a question or for me to repeat something they might have missed the first time.

Lost on Skinwalker Ranch

When I had finished, they were both like "Wow". Dumbfounded.

It wasn't until later that night after taking some shit from Nick that I looked really thin in the face that I stepped on a scale. It had me at 174. I hadn't been under 190 since as long as I could remember. That's when it hit me for real that I had been out there in that canyon for as long as they said I was. I had gone more than three days without food or water wandering lost in some spirit world.

The two scientists were on site before noon that next day. They introduced themselves, and I do remember their names, but the truth is it doesn't matter who they were. I couldn't do any more than tell them the same things I told Nick and Paul. The only difference is they took notes.

Later, we went out to the homestead and I walked them through what I remembered, pointing out where the two coyote-like creatures came through the tree line, how they managed to get me between them and recreating my retreat to the homestead. I told them about the green and purple glow and the orbs, but offered no speculation or explanation. That I left up to them. I told them that when I went into the homestead I was met head-on by some dark shape that rushed into my face, and when I came to—assuming I passed out—I was lying on the chamber floor.

They took it all in objectively, their faces showing interest but otherwise little if any emotion. When they had what they were looking for, they thanked me and said we'd be talking again in Vegas.

I was on a plane by 4:00.

Lost on Skinwalker Ranch

15: The Medicine Man

That's the last time I was at the Ranch. I resigned four weeks later following my last shift in Vegas.

Before that, however, that first week back, they had me reporting to the BAASS building on a daily basis, not to work but to submit to tests—a polygraph, for example, interviews, hypnosis, to answer questions, and they even had me sit with an artist who produced drawings according to what I remembered. He did a damn good job of it, too. I had asked for copies, but they wouldn't give them to me.

Anyway, the whole process had a real scientific feel to it, and as it was all part of the job description and I was getting paid for the full day, I had no complaints.

That said, even to this day, I have never seen any of the results of any of those tests or had the opportunity to read any reports or any of their findings. All I was told was that my recollection of the events while under hypnosis did not differ radically from the way I described things while not under hypnosis—and I passed the polygraph. I was told that while it didn't mean I was telling the truth, it did suggest I wasn't lying.

While I said that I was done with the ranch; the ranch, however, was not done with me.

The very first night back in my apartment I felt that same brooding presence, only this time it was considerably stronger, and though that wet dog smell was probably some sort of psycho-somatic response, I nonetheless couldn't shake it. It was as if it was hanging there just out of reach, but every now and then would sweep just close enough for me to get a whiff.

Lost on Skinwalker Ranch

I went back to sleeping with the bedroom door partially open and the light on out in the hall to create the barrier I knew the presence wouldn't step into or try to cross.

And that wasn't the extent of it. Over the next couple of weeks, my mother started to get that feeling again that someone was at the front door. Go and check and find no one. I didn't notice it myself, but my father made a comment about it, saying that she only did it when I was home. He also complained that she had been waking him almost on a nightly basis, saying she heard footsteps either outside their bedroom or in other parts of the house. Of course, he would get up and find nothing.

When small objects starting going missing and then reappearing in the oddest of places, or when eating utensils and glasses, napkin holders and things like that, left in one place would be found in another, they teased each other for becoming forgetful in their old age. And of course, when she was looking the other way, he would look over at me, tap the side of his head with his index finger and then twirl it around.

However, even he couldn't easily dismiss the coin thing.

Since I was a little kid, he would take the change from his pocket each night and put it in this crystal bowl that my mother had on the top shelf inside the china cabinet in the dining room. When they moved to this house, the china cabinet came along and the routine continued.

On this one night in particular that he told me about, he went to deposit the change only to find a string of coins laid out in a straight line there at the edge and along the full length of the shelf. It was my mother who noticed they had been placed in chronological order according to the date on each.

What else could they believe other than one was playing a practical joke on the other?

The same thing happened two days later, my father walking into the kitchen to make the morning coffee. There were the coins laid out

Lost on Skinwalker Ranch

the length of the counter top of the nook and once again in chronological order. They were left there for me to see.

What could I say? That's when I started to think some kind of professional intervention was in order.

That thought became a certainty on Saturday when I stopped in for a cold one at Ringo's.

I had gone in about four o'clock with the intent of having a couple of cold beers and maybe a shot of Jack. I wasn't planning on staying long as Mom was expecting me for dinner. Ringo and I were the only ones there at the time and we were exchanging the usual small talk. That's when he asked me if I had ever caught up to "that Indian".

I shook my head no and said, "Why do you ask?" I was thinking he had come around, maybe asking for me.

"No reason," he said. "I was opening up this last Wednesday. It was around this time; doesn't make much sense to come in any earlier on a weekday. And as I was sticking the key in the front door, I thought I saw your Indian friend crossing the street up the way a little, going across to the other side. I looked away as I pushed the door open and when I looked back in his direction, he was gone. I looked up and down the block on both sides, thinking maybe he didn't cross and turned back instead. But nothing—a couple of ladies, but no Indian."

"You sure it was him?" I asked, more out of politeness than genuine interest.

He shrugged, "no."

"That reminds me," I said to him, and this time definitely interested. "How'd you make out with that bill he gave you?"

His face took on an instant smirk. "It disappeared."

"You mean like 'vanished'?"

He smirked again, "More like sticky fingers."

I nodded to indicate understanding. "Oh, too bad."

"Someone helped themselves to it. One of my bartenders, if you're asking. Of course, they both swear they know nothing about it. But

Lost on Skinwalker Ranch

it's not like the thing slipped out from underneath the drawer, sprouted wings and flew out the front door on its own."

"That's too bad," I repeated. "I bet that thing was worth a few dollars."

The smirk remained as he said, "I'm sure it was for the one that took it. For what they do for me, I should have just canned them both." He then said, "How about that silver dollar that he left for you? Now that was a pretty thing. Did you ever find out what it was worth?"

The truth of it was that I had forgotten all about that coin—even while asking about the silver certificate. "No, I didn't. In fact, it's sitting in a drawer next to my bed at this very moment. I put it there the same day he gave it to me, and up until now—that you mentioned it—I never gave it another thought. I'm glad you reminded me."

I finished my beer shortly after that, gave an exaggerated look at my watch, thanked Ringo for the shot, left a few dollars and took my leave.

It took some doing, but that next Thursday I had arranged to meet with a man by the name of Aaron Manchester. He was a self-proclaimed Medicine Man, a full-blooded Paiute, living out on the reservation west of my parents.

At first he had no wish to meet with me. The Paiute consider us, meaning white people, unworthy. That's not the best word, perhaps, but let's say when it comes to Indian lore and legend, there's this sense that white people don't take it very seriously. So they are generally suspicious when one of us brings it up.

However, after hearing my story—second hand from a mutual acquaintance—the guy who recommended his services to me in the first place, he agreed.

I had expected difficulty getting on the reservation. But that was not the case. In fact, I even stopped on the way in alongside one of

Lost on Skinwalker Ranch

the reservation cops parked there on the road to ask for directions. He knew exactly who I was asking after and sent me on my way.

I guess I just naturally anticipated some mystical Indian artifacts decorating the front of the house and the yard, but instead all I found was a basic trailer home with white vinyl siding and a wood-rail porch along the length of the front.

As for Aaron Manchester, he was an older man—sixtyish, lean, about my height with long hair, thin, straight and braided, most of it still dark with some narrow streaks of grey to each side. He was dressed in a pair of khaki-colored pants, work boots and a sky-blue, loose-fit button up shirt with a collar.

He met me at the door with a smile and invited me in. We sat in his kitchen and had a couple of cold beers while I told him my story. I covered everything about the ranch, what was going on at the house and meeting Curtis Sammer, the Indian at the bar.

He sat there listening, now and again shaking his head and making faces. I took it as a good sign that he believed what I was saying and that at least parts of it sounded familiar to him.

When I was done, I asked him what he thought.

With a straight-face and rather matter-of-fact, he said I had been targeted by a Skinwalker at the ranch and was lured through a portal. He explained that the coyote-like creatures were a lesser form of Skinwalker, that the spastic movement and mangy bodies told him as much. He called them skin changers, and said that though they were capable of mischief and minor spells, they were more a nuisance than anything else.

His take on the dark entity was altogether different. "That's the one to worry about," he said. "That's the one who touches you even in your home though you are many miles removed. He's that powerful. He's the one we have to deal with."

But before he would get into what that meant exactly, he felt that I needed to be better informed, and as talking was thirsty business, he'd

Lost on Skinwalker Ranch

require a third beer. He insisted I join him. The thought of turning him down never entered my mind.

He got back on topic by telling me about the drawings along the chamber stair. The first ones, he said, were of the Skinwalker, the transformation of man to beast and beast to man. According to him, the Skinwalker is but an imitation of the more ancient and powerful spirit from which the concept was derived.

The second scene was that more ancient and powerful spirit. For some, he said, the lesser figures—the gingerbread men—are thought to represent those from whom the spirit or the soul has recently departed and those upon whom it is yet to be bestowed. It is the Great Spirit that decides.

There are others, however, that hold with a darker interpretation. They believe this entity is malevolent and feeds from the souls of the living, some of whom he enslaves there in the world of half-light and others that he sends out to do his bidding.

The way he explained the silhouettes and shadows was through an analogy of starlight. It was his take that just as the photons of a star long dead continue their journey onward until obstructed, for example by the earth, these too were projections, but of the life force that is in all things; and for some reason, though the flesh has gone, that force yet lingers.

When I asked about the Little People, he had no clear explanation as to who or what they are, or the reason they would have for intervening, seemingly, on my behalf, saying only, "My people have always accepted that these things are part of our world and the harmony within it." But he did not think it far-fetched that it was my body in its physical form that was on that altar.

When we got around to Ringo's, he suggested that the Indian Sammer may have been the Skinwalker as a man, or even one of the Shadow People. He wouldn't know without having seen him. He also said that in all likelihood, that wasn't his name. He called the Skinwalker a deceiver, saying they often use anagrams, changing

Lost on Skinwalker Ranch

around the letters of their real name to make up another. It has something to do with a twisted sense of fair play, allowing the intended victim just enough to avoid the trap—if he's clever enough to see it.

As for the silver coin, it was the entity's attempt, whether Skinwalker or one of the Shadow People, to bind me with a gift. That he did not get me to take it directly, to actually accept it as a gift from his own hand, was the reason, according to Aaron, that its hold on me was not as strong as it otherwise would have been.

Curious as to why Aaron thought this Curtis guy may have been one of the Shadow People, he explained that they, too, are known to tempt mortals with gold and treasure, after which those who give in to the temptation are never heard from again. As for why one of the Shadow People would seek me out, he said only that his people believe when a person is touched by one spirit, he is opened up to others.

When all was said and done, it cost me $250 and one old silver dollar for the Medicine Man to come to my parents' house and my apartment and perform a sort of Native American exorcism. The look on my father's face alone was worth the price. But surprisingly enough, he and my mother went through with it without a fuss. I guess they too were getting tired of midnight footsteps, spoons and forks in the mailbox and levitating coins.

Filling and lighting his "creator's pipe"—as he called it—Aaron drew on the stem over and over again, each time blowing a somewhat sweet, somewhat pungent smoke into every corner of the house, all the while quietly chanting words I couldn't make out, but assumed to be in his native language. When he had finished, he dipped his thumb into the ash and marked the top of all the doorways, inside and out. And as a final touch, placed the ash on my forehead also. He was certain my parents had not been victimized directly, so they didn't get any ashes. His final words were, "What can be done has been done."

Lost on Skinwalker Ranch

Out by his car and before he left, I gave him the silver dollar. He wouldn't take it from me until he got his pipe going again. He then blew a stream of smoke on both sides, wrapped the coin in a white handkerchief he had and pushed into the breast pocket of his shirt. That was the last I saw of Aaron Manchester, Medicine Man.

Believe it or not, his simple ceremony did the trick. That same night, for the first time in weeks, I had no sense of a presence in my apartment. I slept without the light on in the hallway and the whole night through without any strange dreams or unexplained sounds. In the morning, my parents reported no sound of footsteps and Dad's change was in the dish where he had put it the night before.

I continued to provide security at BAASS' local facilities until formally resigning a little more than a week later—although I was told by the home office that I need not return to the ranch in order to keep the job. I decided why tempt fate? –Especially, now that I knew there really is a fate to tempt.

Lost on Skinwalker Ranch

Epilogue

Two years ago, and about two years after my experience at the ranch, I relocated to Peru. I came here after speaking through text and email with a Shaman specializing in the use of ayahuasca. Dealing with personal questions and inner-conflict as a result of my experience on the ranch, I was seeking a sort of spiritual renewal.

Once here, I wound up meeting and socializing with some of the many ex-pats who currently call Peru home. So I rented a small apartment in one of the ex-pat communities and stayed. My parents and my wife—we're still technically married—don't get it, but at the moment that's secondary to my own needs.

What brought me here, like I said, was the Shaman who are among the most gifted guides anywhere in the world when it comes to the use of ayahuasca and bringing the user to the highest spiritual planes possible. For me, it was the only way I could think of to get back to wherever it was that I had crossed over to while on the ranch—at least in the spiritual or psychological sense. I'm afraid even the most talented Shaman and most potent ayahuasca couldn't transport the physical me back to that half-light world into which I had been carried.

But then again, there is no part of me that wants a second confrontation with Skinwalkers or the Shadow People. I'm simply looking for some degree of confirmation that such places exist, as well as portals to pass through. If the ayahuasca can lead me to some place similar, well, that will be evidence enough that where one alternate dimension exists, then another may also.

While my experience to date with the ayahuasca has been positive, and there is no denying the intense synesthesia and psychological effects that come along with the journey, I have yet to find what I'm looking for. Nevertheless, I sleep well at night, and when I am visited

Lost on Skinwalker Ranch

by the stranger at the end of my bed, it is the one with recognizable facial features and not the one black against the darkness.

Printed in Great Britain
by Amazon